THE
STATE OF THE WORLD
ATLAS

Completely Revised and Updated

In memory of
Michael Kidron
1930 – 2003

Also in this series:

THE
STATE OF THE WORLD
ATLAS

Completely Revised and Updated

Dan Smith

with
Ane Bræin

Earthscan Publications Ltd, London

This seventh edition first published in the UK in 2003
by Earthscan Publications Ltd

A catalogue record for this book is available from the British Library
ISBN: 1 84407 029 8

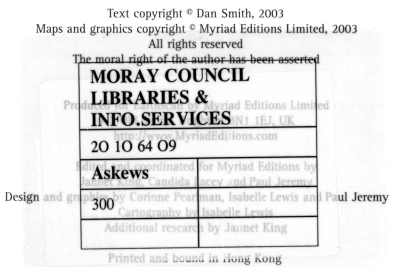

Produced for Earthscan by Myriad Editions Limited
_____ N1 1EJ, UK
http://www.MyriadEditions.com

Edited and coordinated for Myriad Editions by
Jannet King, Candida Lacey and Paul Jeremy

Design and graphics by Corinne Pearlman, Isabelle Lewis and Paul Jeremy
Cartography by Isabelle Lewis

Additional research by Jannet King

Printed and bound in Hong Kong
under the supervision of Bob Cassels, The Hanway Press, London

For a full list of publications please contact:

Earthscan Publications Ltd
120 Pentonville Road, London, N1 9JN, UK
tel: +44 (0)20 7278 0433
fax: +44 (0)20 7278 1142
email: earthinfo@earthscan.co.uk
http://www.earthscan.co.uk

Earthscan is an editorially independent subsidiary of Kogan Page Ltd
and publishes in association with WWF-UK and the International Institute for
Environment and Development.

Contents

The Authors

Dan Smith is a Senior Adviser at, and former Director of, the International Peace Research Institute in Oslo, Norway. He is author of *The Atlas of War and Peace*. His other books include *Pressure: How America runs NATO*. He is also the author of three crime novels. In 2002 Dan Smith was awarded an OBE.

Ane Bræin is the Eastern Mediterranean Project Manager at the International Peace Research Institute in Oslo, Norway. After graduating in Arabic and Middle Eastern Studies, she was a civilian observer with the Temporary International Presence in Hebron. She worked with Dan Smith on *The Atlas of War and Peace*.

Introduction

The world contains some striking anomalies and contrasts, many of which people notice and comment on as a matter of routine as a way of depicting global problems:

- never has there been greater wealth, yet poverty is rife and the gap between richest and poorest shows no sign of closing;
- never has there been more knowledge about more things, yet ignorance and prejudice are also rife and even in the wealthiest countries, many are functionally illiterate;
- the capabilities of science and technology have advanced in recent decades at a rate that defies calm summary – cloning, genetic engineering, information technology and communications, precision mapping of the world, routine flights in outer space – yet the simplest problems often seem to go unsolved.

There are other anomalies that we perhaps comment upon less frequently, yet in which there may be some elements of good news and even grounds for optimism:

- extreme human rights abuse continues, but more is known about it than ever, and some of the most abusive regimes have been overthrown in the past ten to fifteen years;
- economic globalization, which is heading towards the eventual creation of an integrated world market, is flattening out many of the differences between us, yet diversity still flourishes;
- the destruction of the natural environment continues, yet in rich and poor countries alike environmental activism flourishes.

When there are elements of good news, it very often stems from the actions of citizens – ordinary people – who make a stand, either as individuals or in groups, and sometimes in very large numbers, against the decisions of the power-holders. In 1989, in Beijing, China, on the edge Tiananmen Square, in which at the time there was a rally of democratic activists, one man holding a plastic bag stood in front of a tank, and somehow persuaded its driver and commander not to run him down. He hopped backwards and forward and shuffled from side to side and held out his arms from his sides in a sort of blocking motion. And the tank rumbled backwards and forwards but it did not run him down.

Of course, it can be said, it didn't do any good. The army moved in anyway, the activists were shot, beaten or arrested, and a moment of democratic hope in China was extinguished. But the image was a powerful one. One man can stop a tank – one unarmed man. Later that year, people rose up in eastern Europe and pushed repression aside. Regimes that used the language of the rights of people with cruel hypocrisy expected that if the need arose, the USSR would come to their aid. But the USSR had decided not to. And the artificiality and shallowness of their power was exposed and crumbled.

Tiananmen Square and the fall of the Berlin Wall were events the world watched on the television reports. Other actions do not get the same level of global recognition but are just as striking. In the mid-1990s in the UK, the campaign to protect nature and rural peace from new highways was led by individuals who tunnelled under road construction sites so that continuing with the work would put their lives at risk. And road construction in the UK turned out to be like a tank in Beijing – its drivers and directors would not push it forward against that kind of moral stand.

In March 2003 as this atlas was in the closing stages of being prepared for publication, all eyes were on the war on Iraq. The news was not only about the US military build-up, the diplomatic and international political maneuvering for and against the war, and the fighting across the desert and into the streets of Baghdad and Basra. The news was also about the strength of political opposition and public feeling against the war in numerous countries around the world. Some of the views expressed in that wide and deeply felt opposition, perhaps, did not reflect carefully considered judgements; nor, on the other hand, did some of the views expressed by those who favoured and promoted the war. Many opponents of the war were ambivalent about whether their attitude would have been different if the war had been approved beforehand by the UN Security Council – the events in the war would have been more or less the same, but with a different international legal and political context. At the same time, proponents of the war seemed to remain unclear to the end whether the reason for the war was concern about terrorism, or about weapons of mass destruction, or about the unmatched cruelty of the regime of Saddam Hussein – and their opponents disbelieved them on all counts anyway and insisted the real reason for war was oil and a US wish to have strategic control in the Middle East.

Leaving aside the arguments, from one point of view what was most important, at a time when public life seems marked by widespread public indifference, was that people who did not support the approaching war came out and took a visible, public stand.

It is perhaps a further global anomaly that, since the war was fought in part in the name of bringing democracy to Iraq, those who led the war, being democrats, should theoretically have welcomed – not tolerated but positively welcomed – the anti-war opposition.

Democracy is self-evidently a very flawed system of government. The more democratic it is, the more capable it is of inefficiency, with many decisions hard to take and harder to implement. Because of this, even among those who are genuine in their professions of supporting democracy, there can easily be a tendency to take short cuts and circumvent democratic procedures. In some countries, the arrival of democracy since the end of the Cold War has been accompanied by worsening corruption, as a new elite comes on the scene seeking fast-track enrichment. Democracy in many places seems to go along with looser laws and lower standards of political behaviour. The fact that a government or a party or a leader waves the democratic banner around does not mean a great deal.

Despite all this, democracy contains a very attractive fundamental that can be expressed in a single phrase: you might be wrong.

Because those who hold power might be wrong, their views and policies must be subjected to review every now and again. If the verdict is negative, out go the power-holders and some new ones get to try, subject to review in a few years' time. So deep is this assumption in some systems of government, that there are term limits for holders of power, such as the maximum of two four-year terms for the US president. Because of this assumption, to the degree that they are not only democrats but also understand what democracy is about, the holders of power should not just tolerate, but positively welcome, opposition to their policies and actions.

There are several basic conditions that must be met in order for such opposition to exist. First, within the democratic system there has to be a framework of laws protecting rights – freedom of speech and of assembly, freedom to organize, freedom from arbitrary arrest and harassment – and setting procedures so elections are conducted fairly and the actions of government are transparent and accountable. The meta-principle for this framework is equality before the law – the equal worth of every individual, which is also the meta-principle of democracy.

Second, people have to care about issues such as the environment, globalization, war and peace, repression and freedom – and enough people have to care enough to divert energy into doing something about them. There is no forcing people to care, but without the commitment of ordinary citizens, nothing can be done. Often people are unable to find that energy, sometimes because just getting by each day is too much of a struggle already without taking on extra work, but in other circumstances because our upbringing and education do not give us a sense of our responsibilities for each other and for dealing with social and global problems, nor a sense that we can do something about them.

Third, there has to be information available so that the issues can be explained and understood. It is here that this atlas fits in – or, at least, I hope it does. This does not mean that all the information in this atlas supports opposition to governments on a range of important issues. Some does, some does not. Information is like that.

Law-abiding, non-corrupt democratic governments like to get their way, and to do so they have to persuade public opinion, so they marshal the facts, shape them up, and wrap them up in some slogans, backed by more detailed arguments to persuade those whose interest and attention span can absorb more than a brief sound-bite. But information can be inconvenient. Looked at differently, it can support different conclusions. It is, therefore, a democratic principle that there should be a plurality of sources of information and of ways in which the facts are treated.

One thing we do not lack in the wealthier countries is information. But it can be just as bad to get too much information as too little. One of the difficulties is not just to get access to information, but to understand how it fits in – or, perhaps, what it fits into. It is consistently difficult to get to grips with the big picture. The small contribution of this atlas is to try to help the reader understand the big picture.

The maps in this atlas use data that are publicly available and come from reputable organizations; the presentation of the information is designed to be accessible for those who are interested but not necessarily expert. The maps and the graphics are complemented by brief text on each map, highlighting issues of interest. The organization of the atlas is issue-based rather than geographic, and the maps are grouped in eight thematic sections. Each of the eight parts is introduced by some personal comments about the theme.

For my colleague Ane Bræin and me, the task of putting together this atlas came hard on the heels of the completion of the fourth edition of *The Atlas of War and Peace*. I am grateful for her hard work, not only in data gathering and in reviewing the perspectives in the data choices and presentation in the maps, but especially for being a pleasure to work with.

The editorial and design team at Myriad Editions functioned with their usual drive and creativity. I want to thank Paul Jeremy for his early work in conceptualizing the overall shape of the atlas and for his editorial input as the data and design work began. Jannet King made a tremendous contribution as the main editor for this edition and many of the maps owe a great deal to her hard work and determination to get it right. The freshness of the way the information is presented derives from the insight and inventive design work of Corinne Pearlman and Isabelle Lewis. Coordinating and keeping everything on track is Candida Lacey, whose capacity to innovate is as apparently as endless as her energy and good humor. I thank the entire team unreservedly.

Sadly, in March 2003, as we were completing the work on this, the seventh edition of *The State of the World*, Michael Kidron died. Mike was the co-author of the first five editions, together with Ronald Segal.

More than that, he provided much of the initial creative impetus that led to developing this series of atlases that use a variety of visual techniques to present as simply as possible complex information about key world issues. *The State of the World* was the first one in 1982, followed by further atlases about war and peace, gender, environment, health, sexual behaviour, food, the media, smoking, the future, China, water and more to come. People who have found these atlases over the past two decades to be a useful way of gaining some comprehension of the world basically owe it to Mike. And more than that, Mike was a lovely man and great friend who is missed by all those who had the privilege of knowing and working with him. This atlas is dedicated to him with love.

Dan Smith
Athens & Oslo
April 2003

TO UNDERSTAND WHAT IS GOING ON in a world characterized by swift and often fundamental change, it is worth keeping your eye on power. Who gains, who loses – and who seems always to be on the winning side, whatever the game?

It was famously said that all power tends to corrupt and absolute power corrupts absolutely. But it is very rare that power is absolute. Even in most totalitarian regimes, although the power of the rulers is overwhelming and the corruption usually pervasive, there are limits on power and no individual has absolute control. Even in Iraq, a whole section of the country in the north was outside the control of Saddam Hussein's regime in Baghdad, although the Kurds had to pay a heavy price to create that autonomy, and maintained it only with outside help. For the most part, power – whether of rulers or of commercial magnates – is constrained, and the major instrument of that constraint is law.

There is a branch of ethical theory that argues that the reason why we have ethics, and make laws out of ethics, is that cooperation works. In the light of this theory, the strongest, most dynamic, successful and happiest groups, communities, societies and nations are the ones in which people work together most, rather than always competing with each other. Ethics are an expression of that cooperation – treating other people as you yourself would like to be treated, making sure that anything you do does not undermine the general well-being of your group. And then when people do compete in business or in politics or to get good jobs, they do so in a framework of rules that all accept. That, anyway, is the theory.

Only 1 person in 10 thinks that their government responds to the people's will

It is, of course, not that simple in practice. But it doesn't do to be too cynical about ethics and law. Countries in which there is massive corruption are usually economically inefficient, environmentally self-destructive and run by governments that show little practical concern for the welfare of ordinary citizens. Unethical individuals can always get ahead; unethical societies head towards self-destruction. Enron did fine for a long, long time, but if all US companies cooked their books in the same way, American prosperity would not recover from the downturns in the economic cycle that are as inevitable as the boom times. And a world system based on ethics and law would, by definition, be more peaceful than one based on naked power and greed. It is not a bad goal to aim for, whatever degree of confidence you have in the feasibility of achieving it.

Whether it is practical or not, the theory offers some worthwhile insights about power. In any system, the less strong will have more interest in asserting the importance of power and law; the stronger will be more inclined to assert freedom of action. Both may use the language of law and ethics, but it is the less strong who can be counted on to really mean it – not because they are by nature more ethical, but because their self-interest requires an ethical system.

Since the end of the Cold War the USA has become the world's only superpower. It has stretched its military reach across the world to an unprecedented degree. Successive administrations speak the language of democracy, freedom and international law, but from time to time they assume the right to throw off the constraints of international law and act in what they see as US self-interest.

This poses a serious dilemma for the USA. It is undeniably in its self-interest to minimize the restrictions on its freedom of action, just as it is undeniably in the interests of the European states to push steadily for a world that is more and more characterized by respect for effective international law. But for all the many flaws of democracy in the USA over 230 or so years since it was founded, it was the first modern democratic state, and the flow of people migrating to it has remained steady because of the desire for freedom along with prosperity. Democracy, freedom, and equality before the law are deeply embedded in American culture, alongside individualism and the urge for self-betterment. American culture has preferences in both directions – for the rule of law and the rule of the strong.

Which way will the choice go – for international law or for national power? The USA has so much power with which to impose its will on the world that the outcome is of global significance.

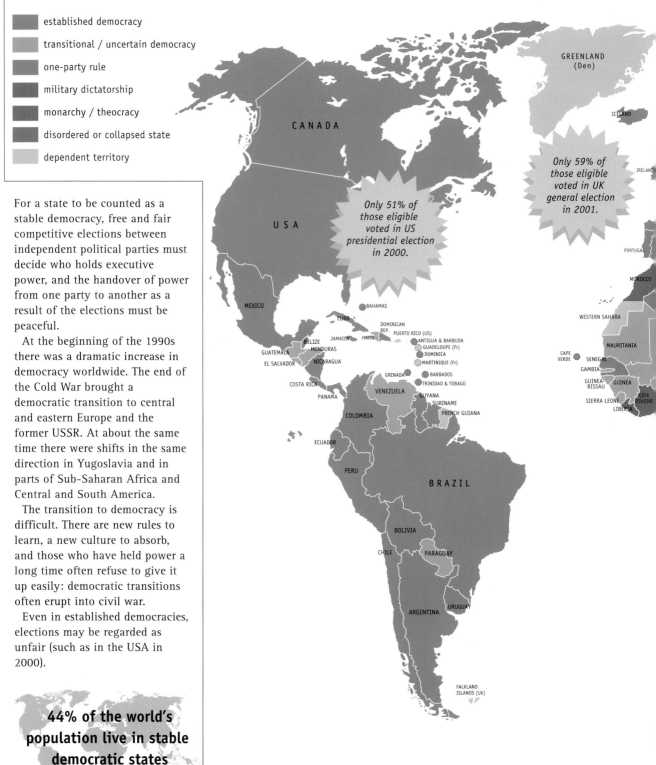

Political systems
2002

- established democracy
- transitional / uncertain democracy
- one-party rule
- military dictatorship
- monarchy / theocracy
- disordered or collapsed state
- dependent territory

For a state to be counted as a stable democracy, free and fair competitive elections between independent political parties must decide who holds executive power, and the handover of power from one party to another as a result of the elections must be peaceful.

At the beginning of the 1990s there was a dramatic increase in democracy worldwide. The end of the Cold War brought a democratic transition to central and eastern Europe and the former USSR. At about the same time there were shifts in the same direction in Yugoslavia and in parts of Sub-Saharan Africa and Central and South America.

The transition to democracy is difficult. There are new rules to learn, a new culture to absorb, and those who have held power a long time often refuse to give it up easily: democratic transitions often erupt into civil war.

Even in established democracies, elections may be regarded as unfair (such as in the USA in 2000).

44% of the world's population live in stable democratic states

Only 51% of those eligible voted in US presidential election in 2000.

Only 59% of those eligible voted in UK general election in 2001.

Political Systems

The more democratic a state, the more political participation it grants to its citizens.

NORWAY
SWEDEN
FINLAND
ESTONIA
LATVIA
LITHUANIA
DENMARK
UNITED KINGDOM
NETH.
BELGIUM
GERMANY
LUX.
POLAND
BELARUS
CZECH REP.
SLOVAKIA
UKRAINE
FRANCE
SWITZ.
AUSTRIA
HUNGARY
MOLDOVA
SLOVENIA
ROMANIA
CROATIA
B.H
YUG
SPAIN
MONACO
ITALY
Kosovo
M
BULGARIA
GEORGIA
ALBANIA
MACEDONIA
GREECE
TURKEY
ARMENIA
AZERBAIJAN
TUNISIA
MALTA
CYPRUS
SYRIA
LEB
IRAQ
ISRAEL
PALESTINE AUTHORITY
JORDAN
KUWAIT
ALGERIA
LIBYA
EGYPT
SAUDI ARABIA
BAHRAIN
QATAR
UAE
OMAN
MALI
NIGER
CHAD
SUDAN
ERITREA
YEMEN
DJIBOUTI
BURKINA FASO
NIGERIA
ETHIOPIA
SOMALIA
BENIN
TOGO
GHANA
CAMEROON
CENTRAL AFRICAN REP.
EQUATORIAL GUINEA
GABON
CONGO
UGANDA
KENYA
DEMOCRATIC REPUBLIC OF CONGO
RWANDA
BURUNDI
TANZANIA
ANGOLA
ZAMBIA
MALAWI
COMOROS
MADAGASCAR
ZIMBABWE
MOZAMBIQUE
NAMIBIA
BOTSWANA
SWAZILAND
SOUTH AFRICA
LESOTHO
SEYCHELLES
MAURITIUS

RUSSIA
KAZAKHSTAN
MONGOLIA
NORTH KOREA
SOUTH KOREA
JAPAN
UZBEKISTAN
KYRGYZSTAN
TURKMENISTAN
TAJIKISTAN
AFGHANISTAN
CHINA
IRAN
PAKISTAN
BHUTAN
NEPAL
INDIA
BANGLADESH
BURMA
TAIWAN
LAOS
VIETNAM
THAILAND
CAMBODIA
PHILIPPINES
SRI LANKA
MALDIVES
BRUNEI
MALAYSIA
SINGAPORE
INDONESIA
EAST TIMOR

KIRIBATI
TUVALU
VANUATU
FRENCH POLYNESIA
FIJI
TONGA
NEW CALEDONIA (Fr)
MICRONESIA
NAURU
PAPUA NEW GUINEA
SOLOMON ISLANDS

AUSTRALIA

NEW ZEALAND

The Law of the Sea
March 2002

Oceans cover 75 percent of the world's surface, hold 90 percent of its water, and contain 97 percent of all life. They are a major natural resource, despite pollution and over-fishing, and are economically vital to many states.

The Convention on the Law of the Sea (1982) recognizes states' sovereignty over the sea up to 12 nautical miles from their coastline, their rights over natural resources up to 200 nautical miles out, known as the Exclusive Economic Zone (EEZ), and control of their part of the continental shelf. With 90 percent of the world's fisheries falling within EEZs landlocked states are economically disadvantaged, although they do have right of access to and through the sea.

The seabed is increasingly being exploited for its natural resources. Offshore drilling produces oil and natural gas, and there are further vast deposits of energy and minerals that will be broached as the necessary technology is developed.

Crime at sea includes piracy and the smuggling of migrants, often in lethally dangerous conditions. Pirates killed 72 merchant sailors in 2000.

About 90% of international trade is transported by sea

Middle East & North Africa 4%

rest of world 14%

rest of Asia 26%

China 11%

Russia 7%

NATO allies 24%

USA 18%

Ownership of warships worldwide
percentage of total
2002

warships 1,240

Control of the Seas

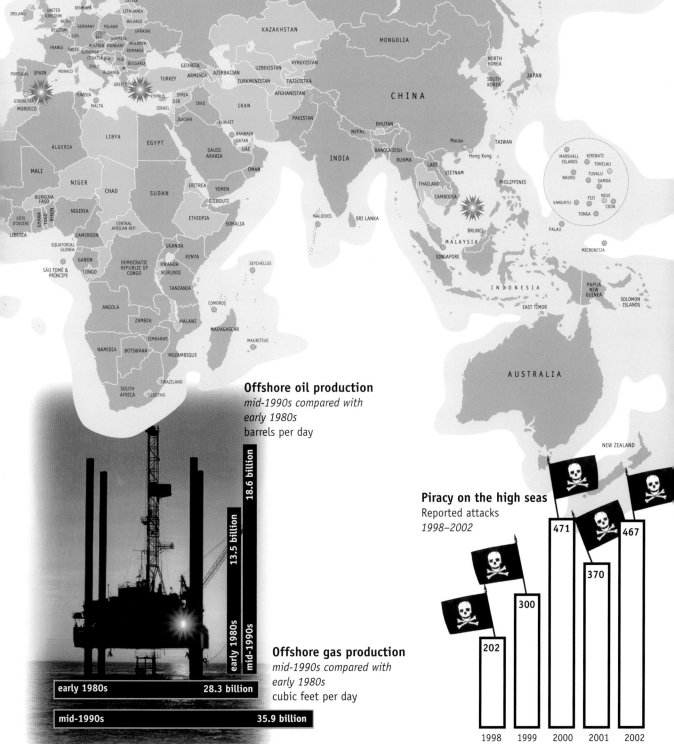

Maritime economic activity – including fishing, offshore oil and gas, transport, tourism and waste disposal – is worth $7,000 billion.

Offshore oil production
mid-1990s compared with early 1980s
barrels per day

18.6 billion
13.5 billion
early 1980s
mid-1990s

Offshore gas production
mid-1990s compared with early 1980s
cubic feet per day

early 1980s   28.3 billion
mid-1990s   35.9 billion

Piracy on the high seas
Reported attacks
1998–2002

1998	1999	2000	2001	2002
202	300	471	370	467

About 10% of all objects launched into space are still functioning

Space is not important because of future possible encounters with other worlds; it is important today because communications and information industries – essential to the technological infrastructure of the modern economy – need satellite technology.

In the 1950s and 1960s, the control of space was seen in terms of manned flights and the race to the moon. It was one of the components of the US–Soviet Cold War. Manned space programs now focus on the International Space Station, which is a cooperative venture between the USA, Russia, Brazil, Canada, Japan and the 15 member states of the European Space Agency. Private corporations are now in the space race, paying for their payloads to be rocketed into space, just as many governments do.

Space-based communication systems have both military and civilian uses. The Global Positioning System, which is funded and controlled by the Pentagon, has thousands of civil users. Linked to a network of ground-based tracking stations, 24 GPS satellites each orbit the earth every 12 hours. The same system helps ships navigate accurately, tracks the migration routes of elks, and guides missiles to their targets.

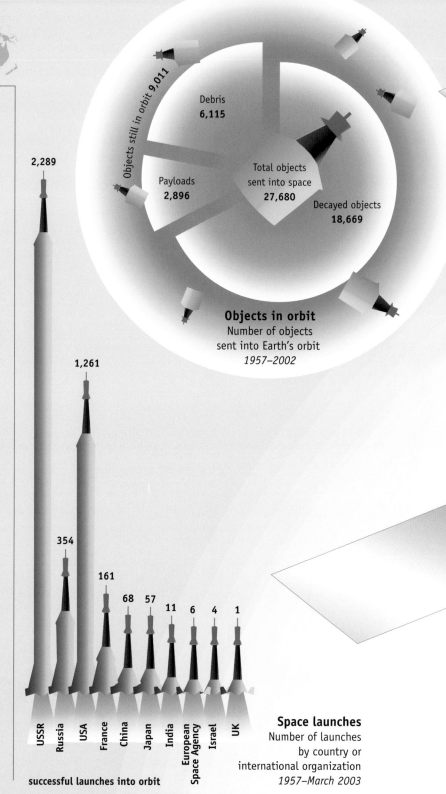

Objects still in orbit **9,011**

Debris
6,115

Payloads
2,896

Total objects
sent into space
27,680

Decayed objects
18,669

Objects in orbit
Number of objects
sent into Earth's orbit
1957–2002

2,289

1,261

354

161

68 57

11 6 4 1

USSR
Russia
USA
France
China
Japan
India
European Space Agency
Israel
UK

successful launches into orbit

Space launches
Number of launches
by country or
international organization
1957–March 2003

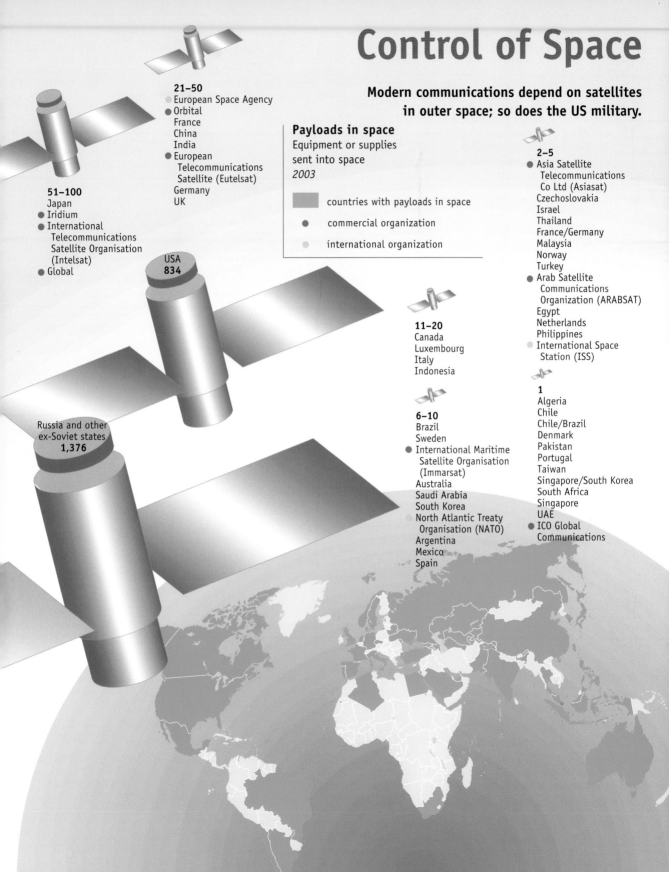

Control of Space

Modern communications depend on satellites in outer space; so does the US military.

21–50
European Space Agency
Orbital
France
China
India
European
Telecommunications
Satellite (Eutelsat)
Germany
UK

51–100
Japan
Iridium
International
Telecommunications
Satellite Organisation
(Intelsat)
Global

Payloads in space
Equipment or supplies
sent into space
2003

countries with payloads in space

commercial organization

international organization

USA
834

Russia and other
ex-Soviet states
1,376

11–20
Canada
Luxembourg
Italy
Indonesia

6–10
Brazil
Sweden
International Maritime
Satellite Organisation
(Immarsat)
Australia
Saudi Arabia
South Korea
North Atlantic Treaty
Organisation (NATO)
Argentina
Mexico
Spain

2–5
Asia Satellite
Telecommunications
Co Ltd (Asiasat)
Czechoslovakia
Israel
Thailand
France/Germany
Malaysia
Norway
Turkey
Arab Satellite
Communications
Organization (ARABSAT)
Egypt
Netherlands
Philippines
International Space
Station (ISS)

1
Algeria
Chile
Chile/Brazil
Denmark
Pakistan
Portugal
Taiwan
Singapore/South Korea
South Africa
Singapore
UAE
ICO Global
Communications

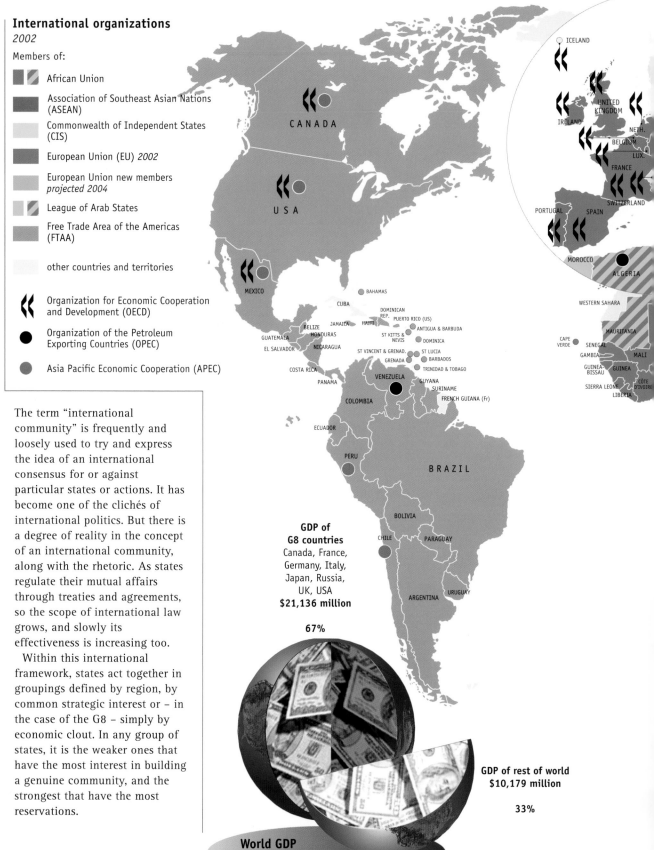

International organizations

2002

Members of:

- African Union
- Association of Southeast Asian Nations (ASEAN)
- Commonwealth of Independent States (CIS)
- European Union (EU) *2002*
- European Union new members *projected 2004*
- League of Arab States
- Free Trade Area of the Americas (FTAA)
- other countries and territories

- Organization for Economic Cooperation and Development (OECD)
- Organization of the Petroleum Exporting Countries (OPEC)
- Asia Pacific Economic Cooperation (APEC)

The term "international community" is frequently and loosely used to try and express the idea of an international consensus for or against particular states or actions. It has become one of the clichés of international politics. But there is a degree of reality in the concept of an international community, along with the rhetoric. As states regulate their mutual affairs through treaties and agreements, so the scope of international law grows, and slowly its effectiveness is increasing too.

Within this international framework, states act together in groupings defined by region, by common strategic interest or – in the case of the G8 – simply by economic clout. In any group of states, it is the weaker ones that have the most interest in building a genuine community, and the strongest that have the most reservations.

GDP of G8 countries
Canada, France, Germany, Italy, Japan, Russia, UK, USA
$21,136 million

67%

GDP of rest of world
$10,179 million

33%

World GDP
$31,315 million

International Organizations

Many states belong to regional organizations through which, with varying degrees of success, they attempt to pursue their economic, political and strategic interests.

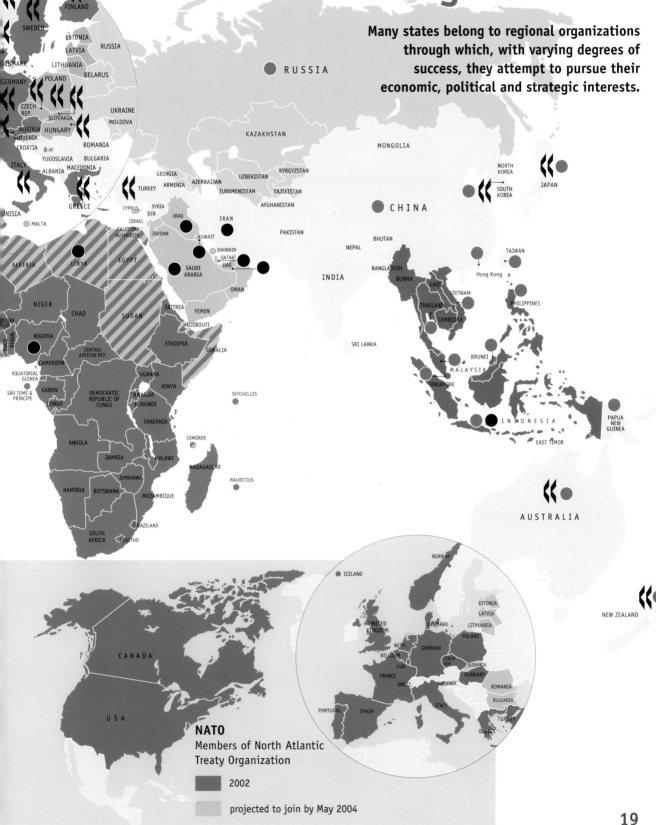

NATO
Members of North Atlantic Treaty Organization

- 2002
- projected to join by May 2004

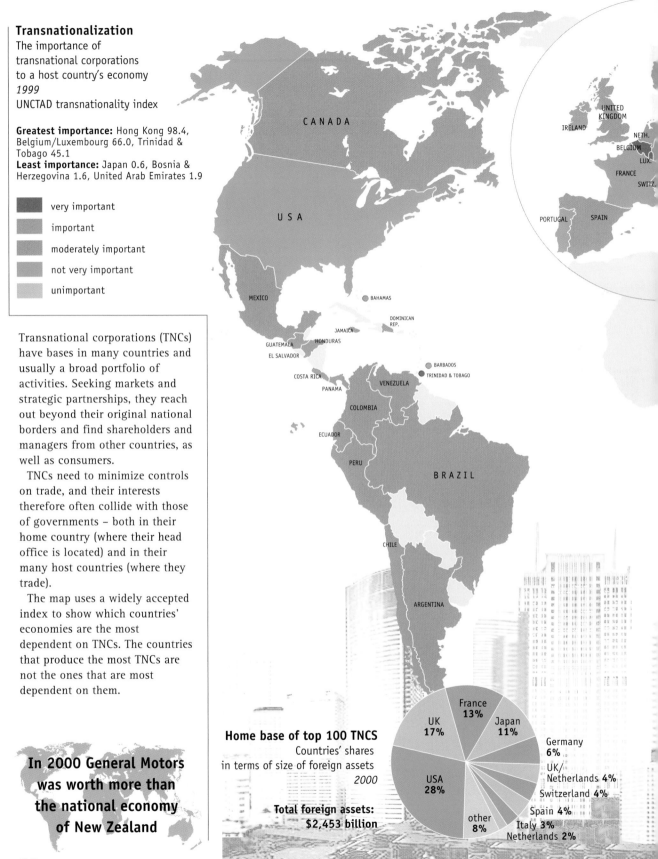

Transnationalization
The importance of
transnational corporations
to a host country's economy
1999
UNCTAD transnationality index

Greatest importance: Hong Kong 98.4,
Belgium/Luxembourg 66.0, Trinidad &
Tobago 45.1
Least importance: Japan 0.6, Bosnia &
Herzegovina 1.6, United Arab Emirates 1.9

- very important
- important
- moderately important
- not very important
- unimportant

Transnational corporations (TNCs) have bases in many countries and usually a broad portfolio of activities. Seeking markets and strategic partnerships, they reach out beyond their original national borders and find shareholders and managers from other countries, as well as consumers.

TNCs need to minimize controls on trade, and their interests therefore often collide with those of governments – both in their home country (where their head office is located) and in their many host countries (where they trade).

The map uses a widely accepted index to show which countries' economies are the most dependent on TNCs. The countries that produce the most TNCs are not the ones that are most dependent on them.

In 2000 General Motors was worth more than the national economy of New Zealand

Home base of top 100 TNCS
Countries' shares
in terms of size of foreign assets
2000

Total foreign assets:
$2,453 billion

France **13%**
Japan **11%**
UK **17%**
USA **28%**
Germany **6%**
UK/ Netherlands **4%**
Switzerland **4%**
Spain **4%**
Italy **3%**
Netherlands **2%**
other **8%**

Transnational Corporations

Globalization of the world economy is not new, but it is further advanced now than ever before. The interests and loyalties of transnational corporations reach beyond national interests and loyalties.

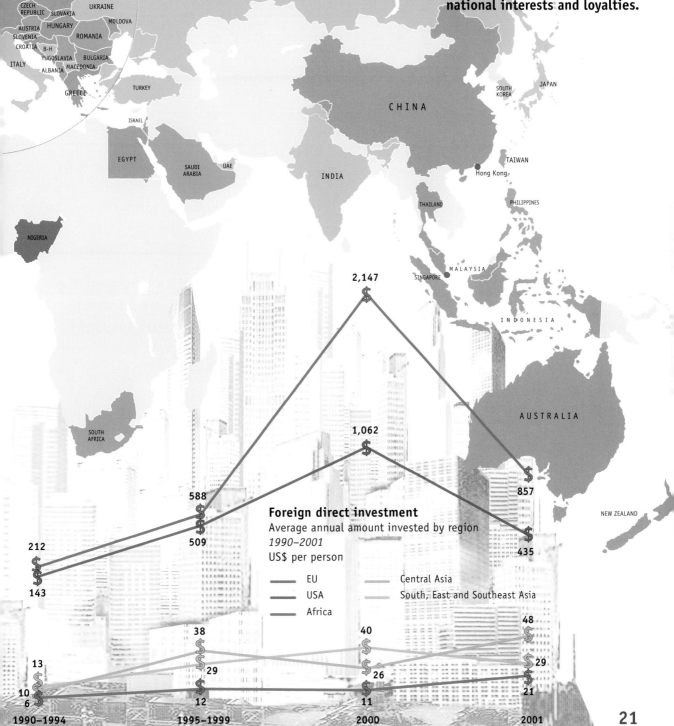

Foreign direct investment
Average annual amount invested by region
1990–2001
US$ per person

- EU
- USA
- Africa
- Central Asia
- South, East and Southeast Asia

2,147

1,062

857

588

509

435

212

143

48

40

38

29

29

26

21

13

12

11

10

6

1990–1994   1995–1999   2000   2001

US friends and foes

2002

- USA and territories
- core ally
- states with security/political ties/agreements with USA
- uncertain friends and allies
- unfriendly states
- states declared by US president to be "axis of evil"
- other states

US forces abroad

2002

US military presence:

- over 10,000 US military personnel
- 1,000 – 10,000 US military personnel
- up to 1,000 US military personnel

US forces in peacekeeping operations:

- 1,000 – 10,000 US military personnel
- up to 1,000 US military personnel

No other power has such advanced weaponry as the USA or the ability to deploy it all round the world. No other power has such a network of military bases worldwide or such large numbers of highly trained military personnel. And since the suicide attacks on the World Trade Center and Pentagon on September 11, 2001, the USA has been more prepared to use this unrivalled power than at any time since the withdrawal from Vietnam in 1973, and to suffer the casualties in war that even a superpower must inevitably suffer.

In the wake of 9/11, US forces returned to the Philippines, increased in number in the Gulf and Middle East, and deployed in Afghanistan and Central Asia for the first time. This extended presence brings extended power, but at the same extended vulnerability. Like American embassies, US bases may present tempting targets for 9/11-type attackers. A full debate in the USA about the costs and benefits of US power for ordinary Americans has not yet happened.

The controversy in the UN Security Council in early 2003 about the war on Iraq and the many enormous demonstrations against the war showed, however, that there is an impassioned debate about the impact of US power on the world.

RUSSIA

CHINA

NORTH KOREA

SOUTH KOREA

JAPAN

TAIWAN

Hong Kong

THAILAND

PHILIPPINES

MALAYSIA

SINGAPORE

INDONESIA

EAST TIMOR

AUSTRALIA

NEW ZEALAND

The USA is responsible for 40% of world military spending

Superpower

Following the end of the Cold War, the USA has become the world's only superpower.

GREENLAND (Den)
ICELAND
NORWAY
FINLAND
SWEDEN
ESTONIA
LATVIA
RUSSIA
IRELAND
UNITED KINGDOM
DENMARK
LITHUANIA
NETH.
BELGIUM
GERMANY
POLAND
BELARUS
LUX.
CZECH REPUBLIC
SLOVAKIA
UKRAINE
FRANCE
SWITZ.
AUSTRIA
HUNGARY
MOLDOVA
SLOVENIA
ROMANIA
YUGOSLAVIA
ITALY
B-H
CROATIA
ALB.
MACEDONIA
BULGARIA
GREECE
PORTUGAL
SPAIN
MOROCCO

RUSSIA
KAZAKHSTAN
GEORGIA
AZERBAIJAN
UZBEKISTAN
KYRGYZSTAN
TURKEY
ARMENIA
TURKMENISTAN
TAJIKISTAN
SYRIA
IRAQ
IRAN
AFGHANISTAN
ISRAEL
JORDAN
PAKISTAN
INDIA
see inset

CANADA
USA
MEXICO
BAHAMAS
CUBA
JAMAICA
HAITI
DOMINICAN REP.
PUERTO RICO (US)
ANTIGUA & BARBUDA
ST KITTS & NEVIS
GUADELOUPE (Fr)
DOMINICA
MARTINIQUE (Fr)
BARBADOS
GRENADA
TRINIDAD & TOBAGO
BELIZE
GUATEMALA
HONDURAS
EL SALVADOR
NICARAGUA
COSTA RICA
PANAMA
VENEZUELA
GUYANA
FRENCH GUIANA (Fr)
COLOMBIA
ECUADOR
PERU
BRAZIL
BOLIVIA
PARAGUAY
CHILE
URUGUAY
ARGENTINA
FALKLAND ISLANDS (UK)

BERMUDA (UK)

WESTERN SAHARA
MOROCCO
LIBYA
EGYPT
NIGER
SUDAN
NIGERIA
LIBERIA
ETHIOPIA
ZIMBABWE
DIEGO GARCIA (UK)

March 2002
150,000 US troops assembled in The Gulf region ready for attack on Iraq.

KUWAIT
BAHRAIN
QATAR
UAE
SAUDI ARABIA
ERITREA
OMAN

Part 2

The Cost of Living

THE FITNESS ENTHUSIAST'S STANDARD MOTTO – "No gain without pain" – seems to apply to worldwide social and economic development. All the statistics show that economic development keeps on advancing as new technologies come through and more and more wealth is produced. But everything comes at a cost and all round us we can see the pain of progress.

As the 20th century came to an end, awareness increased of the extent to which economic activity is damaging the natural environment. There are serious disagreements and arguments about how to interpret some of the data, and especially about whether and how to extrapolate long-term trends from the data of the past two decades. There is in particular a continuing controversy about whether global warming is actually occurring, or whether the increase in average temperatures worldwide in the closing decades of the 20th century was a normal fluctuation such as the world has often seen before. Overall, however, there is no major disagreement that serious harm has been inflicted on the natural environment, that the oceans are increasingly polluted, forests stripped bare, that species of animal and plant life are threatened with extinction, that the ozone layer has thinned out in several places, and that the ice caps are shrinking. Nor is there serious disagreement with the scientific conclusions on the long-term effects of emissions of carbon dioxide and other gases.

The difficulty does not seem to be in understanding what is going on. The facts are there and the risks are clear. Instead, the difficulty is about getting agreement on what to do. Environmentalists' proposals for adopting worldwide regulations to restrict emissions of the so-called greenhouse gases that would lead to global warming were diluted time and again before agreement could be reached on a global treaty – the Kyoto Treaty – which was effectively set aside because of US opposition. The result is that, in the face of a looming peril, the decision was to do nothing. Each year of doing nothing does not simply defer the solution, it makes the problem worse.

It is a widely cited if gruesome fact that, apparently, if you throw a frog into a pan of boiling water it will jump straight out to save itself, but if you put it in cold water which you slowly heat, the frog will stay there until it boils to death. The big question that is posed to humanity in general, and governments in particular, is quite simple: are you smarter than a frog?

Not all the developments are all bad. Population growth, for example, is a product of prosperity up to a certain point, because of better sanitation and medical technologies, but as economic growth continues population growth slows down. Today, after decades of worrying about a nightmare future of intense over-crowding and over-population, some demographers are predicting global population decline late in the 21st century. This raises the problem for many countries of an ageing population, in which the economically active people have to support a growing number of senior citizens who do not go out to work. To deal with that problem should not be beyond human ingenuity as long as people and their governments think far enough ahead – another example of the frog question.

Likewise, energy consumption may not be the problem it is made out to be. Precisely because energy is fundamental, it is unthinkable that profit-oriented enterprise will neglect future energy needs. Governments might be frog-like but corporations will probably be more far-sighted. Moreover, there are many alternative sources of energy and the technologies to harness it – from the tides and waves of the sea, from wind and sun, and from technologies that may be just around the corner, such as fusion, which could be a cheaper energy source than nuclear fission with its radioactive waste.

If the human frog can get itself together and not only see danger coming, but understand and act on the need to do something about the future disaster today, there are other challenges that have as yet been barely taken on. Urban life for many tens of millions of people is a nightmare of polluted air, cramped living quarters with neither privacy nor cleanliness, with polluted water supplies and inadequate sewage systems. As we attempt to undo some of the damage that has been done to the natural environment, there needs also to be an effort to make urban life sustainable.

Four times as many people lived in cities in 2000 as in 1950

Population size
Countries' share of world population

- ☐ = 1%
- ◻ = 0.1%
- ▫ = 0.01%

Population change
Rate of annual change
2002

- 3% increase or more
- 2% – 2.9% increase
- 1% – 1.9% increase
- under 1% increase
- decrease

The world's population doubled in the second half of the 20th century, passing 6 billion at the start of the 21st. The rate of growth has slowed, especially in the two most populous countries – China and India – but on current trends the total will top 9 billion in 2050, with Africa and parts of the Middle East growing fastest.

As population growth slows and even declines in the richer countries, the average age rises. Then, the economically active must support not only themselves but a rising number of older people. The result is a looming welfare crisis.

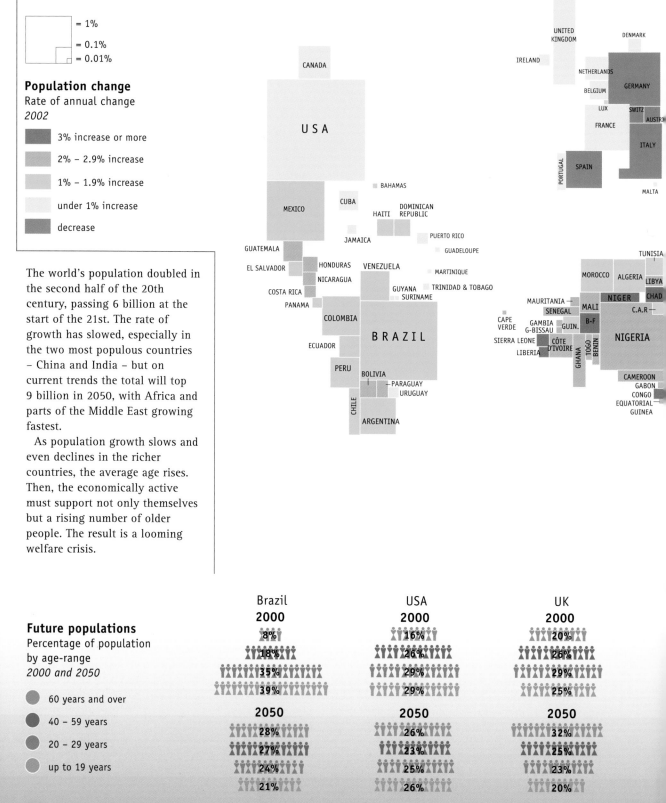

Future populations
Percentage of population by age-range
2000 and 2050

- 60 years and over
- 40 – 59 years
- 20 – 29 years
- up to 19 years

Brazil
2000
8%
18%
35%
39%
2050
28%
27%
24%
21%

USA
2000
16%
26%
29%
29%
2050
26%
23%
25%
26%

UK
2000
20%
26%
29%
25%
2050
32%
25%
23%
20%

Population

As countries get richer, the population grows more slowly.

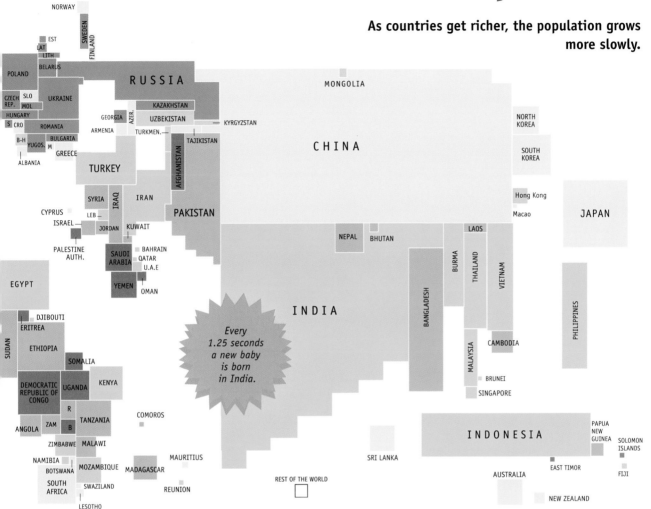

NORWAY
EST
LAT
LITH
SWEDEN
FINLAND
POLAND
BELARUS
RUSSIA
CZECH REP.
SLO
MOL
UKRAINE
KAZAKHSTAN
KYRGYZSTAN
HUNGARY
S CRO
ROMANIA
GEORGIA
AZER.
UZBEKISTAN
MONGOLIA
B-H YUGOS. M
BULGARIA
ARMENIA
TURKMEN.
TAJIKISTAN
ALBANIA
GREECE
AFGHANISTAN
NORTH KOREA
TURKEY
CHINA
SOUTH KOREA
SYRIA
IRAQ
IRAN
CYPRUS
LEB
PAKISTAN
Hong Kong
Macao
JAPAN
ISRAEL
JORDAN
KUWAIT
PALESTINE AUTH.
BAHRAIN
QATAR
U.A.E
NEPAL
BHUTAN
LAOS
EGYPT
SAUDI ARABIA
YEMEN
OMAN
BANGLADESH
BURMA
THAILAND
VIETNAM
DJIBOUTI
ERITREA
ETHIOPIA
SOMALIA
INDIA
MALAYSIA
PHILIPPINES
SUDAN
UGANDA
KENYA
CAMBODIA
DEMOCRATIC REPUBLIC OF CONGO
R
BRUNEI
SINGAPORE
ANGOLA
ZAM
B
TANZANIA
COMOROS
ZIMBABWE
MALAWI
INDONESIA
PAPUA NEW GUINEA
SOLOMON ISLANDS
NAMIBIA
MAURITIUS
SRI LANKA
EAST TIMOR
FIJI
BOTSWANA
MOZAMBIQUE
MADAGASCAR
AUSTRALIA
SOUTH AFRICA
SWAZILAND
REUNION
REST OF THE WORLD
NEW ZEALAND
LESOTHO

Every 1.25 seconds a new baby is born in India.

Nigeria	Egypt	India	Russia
2000	**2000**	**2000**	**2000**
4%	6%	7%	18%
13%	17%	17%	27%
28%	31%	32%	29%
55%	46%	44%	26%
2050	**2050**	**2050**	**2050**
8%	20%	20%	35%
20%	26%	26%	24%
33%	27%	27%	23%
39%	27%	27%	18%

People living in cities

As a percentage of
total population
2000

- over 80%
- 61% – 80%
- 41% – 60%
- 21% – 40%
- 20% and under
- no data

Megacities?

2000 and 2015 projected

- city with population over 10 million in 2000
- city projected to have population over 10 million in 2015

Richer countries tend to have a larger proportion of city dwellers than the poorer countries. In some countries in South America, however, more people are packed into cities than the average for North America or parts of Europe – without the same level of wealth. The result is the huge shanty towns and *favelas* of the urban poor.

While the number of megacities looks set to increase, improved transport and communications are reducing the need to concentrate people in a few places. In the 1990s economic boom, it was mainly the smaller cities that were the most economically dynamic.

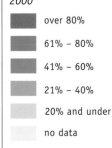

Nearly half of the world's population live in cities

Urban populations

by region
2000

North America
243 million
8%

Oceania
23 million
1%

Africa
295 million
10%

Latin America & Caribbean
391 million
14%

Total 2,861 million

Asia
1,376 million
48%

Europe
534 million
19%

Urbanization

The proportion of people living in cities looks set to grow from 40 percent in 1980 to 60 percent in 2020.

Urban populations in 2015
Projected percentage increase by region
2000–2015

- Asia — 46%
- Europe — 1%
- Latin America & Caribbean — 30%
- Africa — 71%
- North America — 19%
- Oceania — 15%

Motor vehicles

Number per 1,000 people
2000 or latest available data

■	over 500
■	251 – 500
■	101 – 250
■	11 – 100
■	0 – 10
■	no data

Congestion

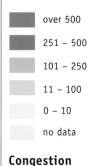

53 over 50 motor vehicles
per kilometer of main road
number given

Road transport plays a vital role in the economy and lifestyle of the richer nations, increasing their reliance on oil – a major factor in international politics.

The car was the first major consumer product to be mass-marketed, and was the basis of the USA's economic growth and industrial pre-eminence.

Cars are a relatively affordable, convenient and private means of transport, providing users with independence. They are also a more dangerous means of transport than buses, trains or aircraft, and create more air pollution, greenhouse gas emissions and noise.

The increasing number of private cars and road freight is leading to severe congestion in some industrialized countries. In the developing world, where an increase in motor vehicles is not linked to an improved infra-structure, the high proportion of road deaths is a growing problem.

62 NETHERLANDS
58
UNITED KINGDOM
IRELAND
BELGIUM
FRANCE
54
PORTUGAL SPAIN SWITZERLAND
53
MOROCCO

CANADA
USA
MEXICO
CUBA
DOMINICAN REP.
GUATEMALA HONDURAS
EL SALVADOR NICARAGUA
COSTA RICA
PANAMA
COLOMBIA
ECUADOR
PERU
BRAZIL
BOLIVIA
CHILE
62
URUGUAY
ARGENTINA

MAURITANIA
SENEGAL
GAMBIA MALI
GUINEA-BISSAU GUINEA
CÔTE D'IVOIRE
SIERRA LEONE
LIBERIA

161
Nigeria

55
Kenya

Relative safety

Number of road deaths
per 10,000 motor vehicles
1990s

1
Norway

2
Australia, Canada, Finland, Germany, Italy, Japan, UK, USA

3
France, Madagascar, New Zealand, Spain

6
Greece, Hungary, Iran, Malaysia

15
Korea, Chile, Russia

25
Burkina Faso, India

26
China, Zimbabwe

By 2030, on current trends, 2.5 million people each year will die from traffic accidents in developing countries.

Traffic

The world's car population has grown five times as fast as the human population over the last 50 years.

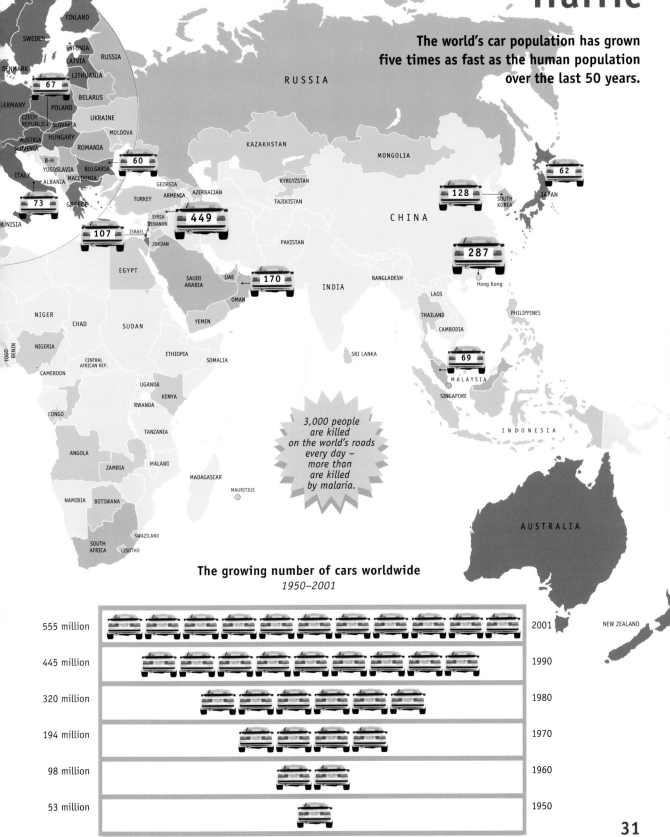

NORWAY
FINLAND
SWEDEN
ESTONIA
DENMARK
LATVIA
LITHUANIA
RUSSIA
BELARUS
GERMANY
CZECH REPUBLIC
POLAND
SLOVAKIA
UKRAINE
MOLDOVA
AUSTRIA
HUNGARY
SLOVENIA
ROMANIA
B-H
YUGOSLAVIA
BULGARIA
ITALY
ALBANIA
MACEDONIA
TUNISIA
GEORGIA
GREECE
ARMENIA
AZERBAIJAN
TURKEY
SYRIA
LEBANON
ISRAEL
JORDAN
EGYPT
SAUDI ARABIA
UAE
OMAN
YEMEN
NIGER
CHAD
SUDAN
NIGERIA
CENTRAL AFRICAN REP.
ETHIOPIA
SOMALIA
TOGO
BENIN
CAMEROON
CONGO
UGANDA
KENYA
RWANDA
TANZANIA
ANGOLA
ZAMBIA
MALAWI
MADAGASCAR
MAURITIUS
NAMIBIA
BOTSWANA
SWAZILAND
SOUTH AFRICA
LESOTHO

RUSSIA
KAZAKHSTAN
MONGOLIA
KYRGYZSTAN
TAJIKISTAN
CHINA
PAKISTAN
INDIA
BANGLADESH
LAOS
THAILAND
CAMBODIA
SRI LANKA
MALAYSIA
SINGAPORE
PHILIPPINES
INDONESIA
JAPAN
SOUTH KOREA
Hong Kong

AUSTRALIA
NEW ZEALAND

67
60
73
107
449
170
62
128
287
69

3,000 people are killed on the world's roads every day – more than are killed by malaria.

The growing number of cars worldwide
1950–2001

555 million	2001
445 million	1990
320 million	1980
194 million	1970
98 million	1960
53 million	1950

31

Energy consumption

Average energy used per person
2000
unit equal to energy produced
by a tonne of oil

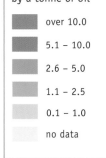

- over 10.0
- 5.1 – 10.0
- 2.6 – 5.0
- 1.1 – 2.5
- 0.1 – 1.0
- no data

Energy can be bought, sold and fought over. It is a highly varied and wholly essential commodity, without which nothing can be done.

As countries get richer they consume more energy per person, until their economies shift from manufacturing to the information and service sectors. Then, energy efficiency increases and consumption tends to decline.

Almost all energy consumed comes from coal, gas, oil or uranium. These non-renewable energy sources create pollution, risk major accidents, and cannot be sustained in the long term.

Renewable energy sources – using the power of the wind, waves and sun as well as hydro-electricity – are being used in some countries. They could be used worldwide when companies find them more profitable, or when governments opt for safer energy.

Over 90% of energy used comes from non-renewable sources

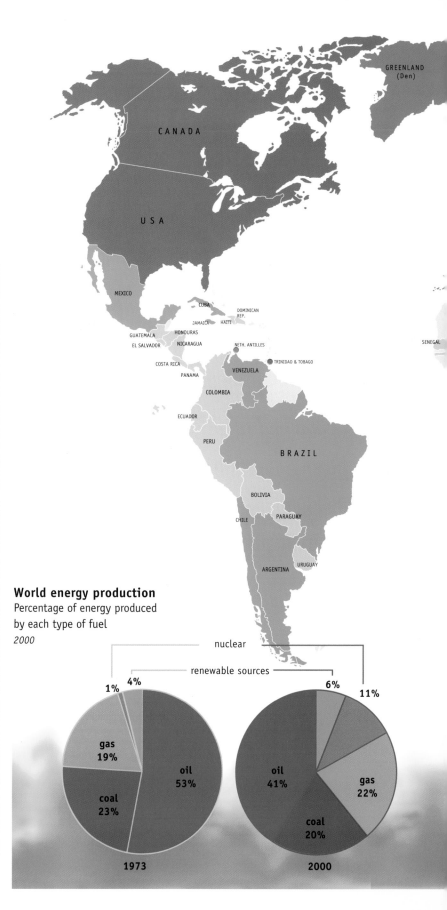

World energy production

Percentage of energy produced
by each type of fuel
2000

nuclear

renewable sources

1973

- 1%
- 4%
- gas 19%
- oil 53%
- coal 23%

2000

- 6%
- 11%
- oil 41%
- gas 22%
- coal 20%

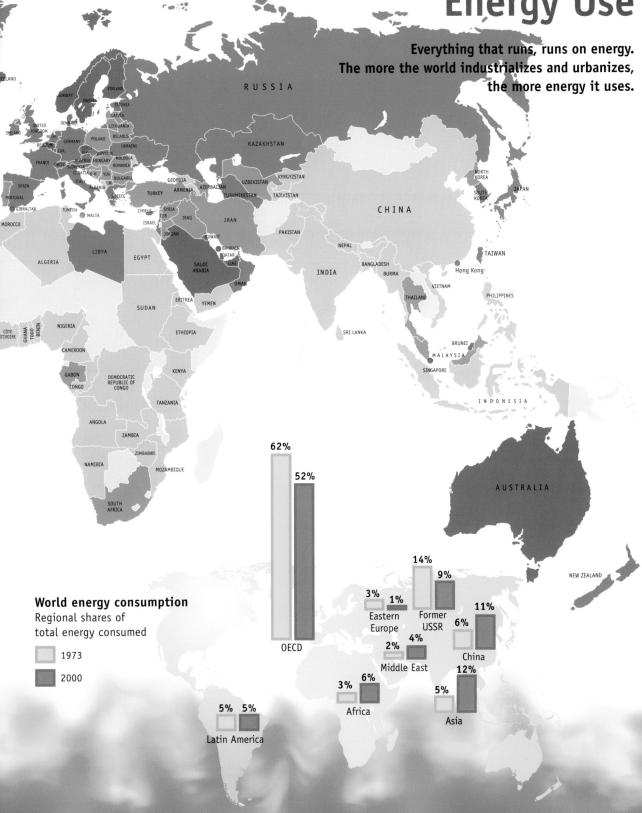

Energy Use

Everything that runs, runs on energy.
The more the world industrializes and urbanizes,
the more energy it uses.

World energy consumption
Regional shares of
total energy consumed

- 1973
- 2000

OECD — 62% / 52%

Eastern Europe — 3% / 1%

Former USSR — 14% / 9%

Middle East — 2% / 4%

China — 6% / 11%

Africa — 3% / 6%

Asia — 5% / 12%

Latin America — 5% / 5%

Greenhouse gases

Countries' shares of world carbon dioxide emissions
2000
countries emitting 0.1% or more
of world total
World total: 22.7 billion tonnes a year

☐ = 1%

☐ = 0.1%

Annual emissions of CO_2
per person
2000
tonnes

- 15 and over
- 10.0 – 14.9
- 5.0 – 9.9
- under 5

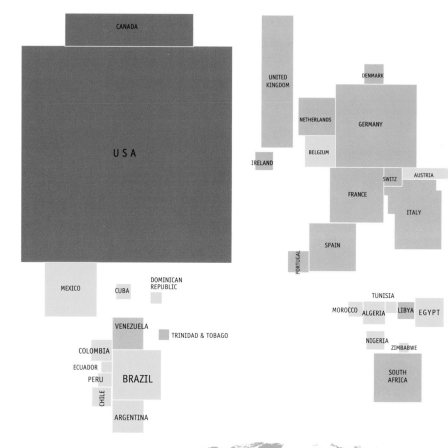

Increasing energy use causes greater emissions of greenhouse gases – of which the most important is carbon dioxide (CO_2). The destruction of forests (see pages 36–37) means less CO_2 is absorbed by trees.

If the current increase in average temperatures continues, it will cause major climate change, reducing rainfall in some areas and increasing it in others. This will affect natural habitats worldwide, and will probably lead to the extinction of many species. There is also the risk of the Arctic and Antarctic ice caps melting, which would cause sea levels to rise, flooding small islands and low-lying coastal areas.

The fact that there have always been large temperature fluctuations over long time periods is used by some governments as an excuse for inaction.

Global warming

Increase in average annual global temperature
1991–2002
compared with average for
1961–1990
degrees centigrade

Every year, between 1991 and 2002, was warmer than the annual average for the previous 30 years

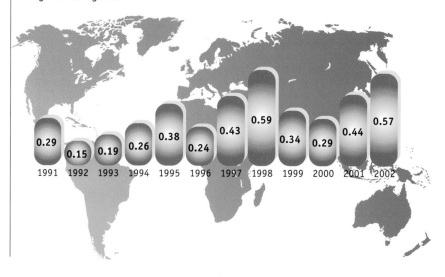

1991 0.29
1992 0.15
1993 0.19
1994 0.26
1995 0.38
1996 0.24
1997 0.43
1998 0.59
1999 0.34
2000 0.29
2001 0.44
2002 0.57

Climate Change

World temperatures appear to be rising, but whether this is a result of the greenhouse effect remains controversial.

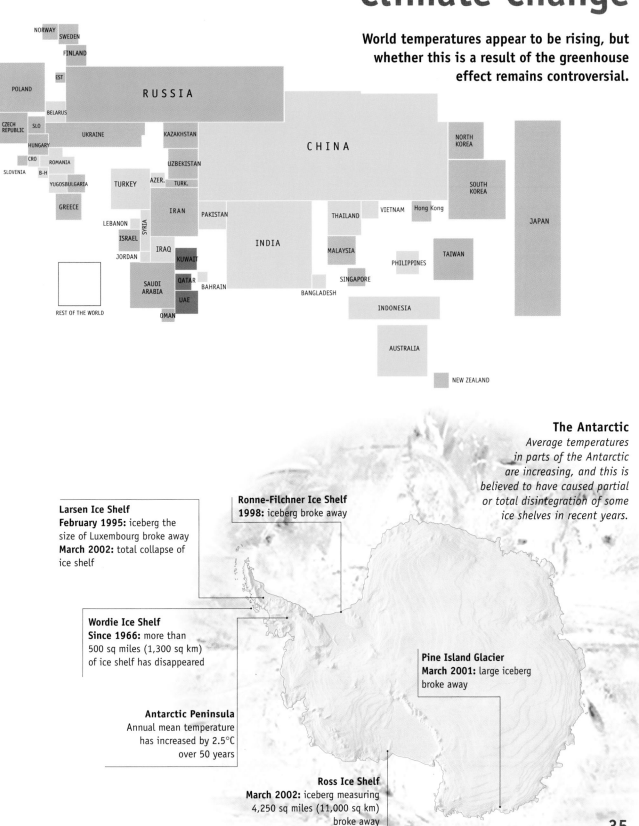

NORWAY
SWEDEN
FINLAND
EST
POLAND
RUSSIA
BELARUS
CZECH REPUBLIC
SLO
UKRAINE
KAZAKHSTAN
HUNGARY
CRO
ROMANIA
SLOVENIA
B-H
YUGOS
BULGARIA
UZBEKISTAN
CHINA
NORTH KOREA
GREECE
TURKEY
AZER.
TURK.
SOUTH KOREA
LEBANON
IRAN
PAKISTAN
THAILAND
VIETNAM
Hong Kong
JAPAN
ISRAEL
SYRIA
JORDAN
IRAQ
KUWAIT
INDIA
MALAYSIA
TAIWAN
REST OF THE WORLD
SAUDI ARABIA
QATAR
BAHRAIN
UAE
OMAN
BANGLADESH
SINGAPORE
PHILIPPINES
INDONESIA
AUSTRALIA
NEW ZEALAND

The Antarctic
Average temperatures in parts of the Antarctic are increasing, and this is believed to have caused partial or total disintegration of some ice shelves in recent years.

Larsen Ice Shelf
February 1995: iceberg the size of Luxembourg broke away
March 2002: total collapse of ice shelf

Ronne-Filchner Ice Shelf
1998: iceberg broke away

Wordie Ice Shelf
Since 1966: more than 500 sq miles (1,300 sq km) of ice shelf has disappeared

Pine Island Glacier
March 2001: large iceberg broke away

Antarctic Peninsula
Annual mean temperature has increased by 2.5°C over 50 years

Ross Ice Shelf
March 2002: iceberg measuring 4,250 sq miles (11,000 sq km) broke away

35

Forests

Average annual percentage
change in natural forest
1990–2000

Loss of:

- over 2.5%
- 0.1% – 2.4%
- no change

Gain of:

- 0.1% – 2.4%
- over 2.5%
- no data

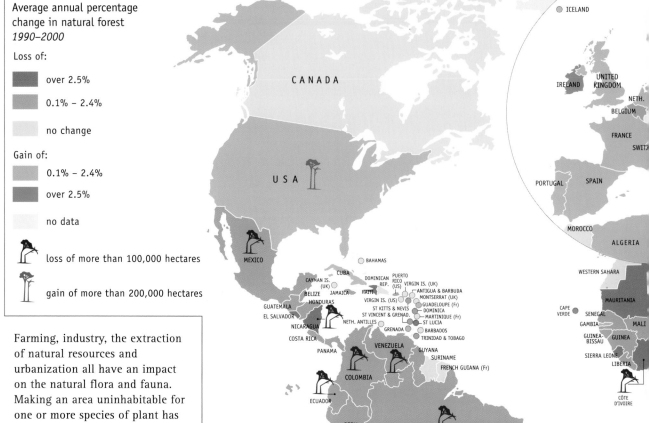

loss of more than 100,000 hectares

gain of more than 200,000 hectares

Farming, industry, the extraction
of natural resources and
urbanization all have an impact
on the natural flora and fauna.
Making an area uninhabitable for
one or more species of plant has
an impact on insects, birds,
reptiles and mammals along the
food chain.

Logging is especially damaging.
Forests hold soil to the ground
and regulate the water supply to
the surrounding region. They are
part of the climate system and are
home to a rich variety of wildlife.
Without a strategy for replacing
trees, permanent damage is
inflicted.

The rate at which forest is being
lost is slowing – partly because of
international concern, partly
because in many places there is
little forest left to cut down – but
the pressure remains. For many
poor countries, hardwood is the
main reliable source of the hard
currency needed to repay
international debts.

**1.7 million species
have been identified
– less than 10%
of the likely total**

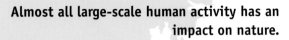

Biodiversity

Almost all large-scale human activity has an impact on nature.

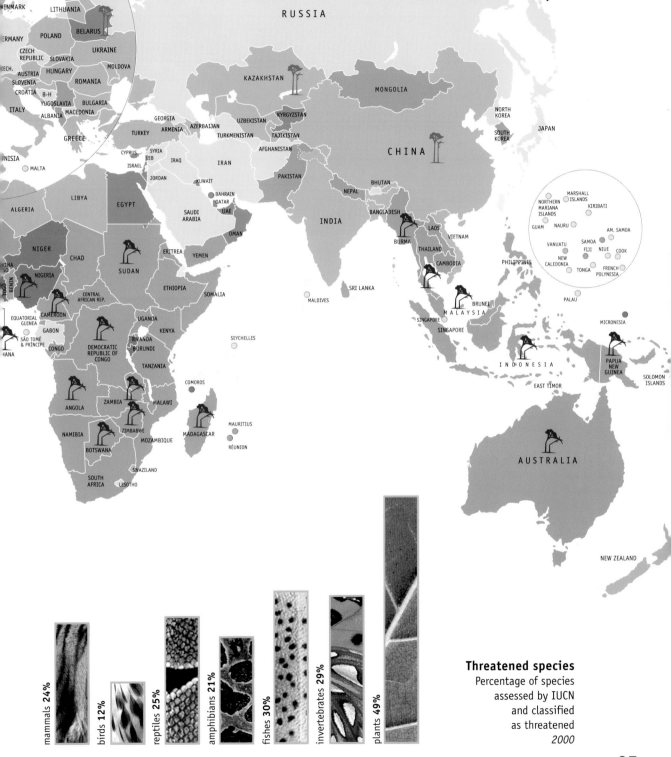

Threatened species
Percentage of species
assessed by IUCN
and classified
as threatened
2000

mammals **24%**

birds **12%**

reptiles **25%**

amphibians **21%**

fishes **30%**

invertebrates **29%**

plants **49%**

Water use

Total water used for industry, agriculture and domestic uses
2002 or latest available data
liters per person per day

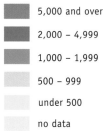

- 5,000 and over
- 2,000 – 4,999
- 1,000 – 1,999
- 500 – 999
- under 500
- no data

Highest: Turkmenistan 13,752
Lowest: Democratic Republic of Congo 19

Water scarcity

under 2,700 liters of water available per person per day (excluding desalinated water)

Water dependency

75% or more of available water originates from outside country

Water use varies widely according to its availability, its importance to a country's industry or agriculture, and the way in which people use it in their homes.

Water is one of the basic requirements for life, and it is becoming more and more scarce as a result of population increase and climate change. Commercial companies are buying exclusive rights to rivers and aquifers, often in areas where the local people are chronically short of water.

Power struggles over water are increasingly likely to be the cause of conflict. The destruction or contamination of water supplies is itself a weapon of war. In the Gulf War in 1991 Iraq destroyed Kuwait's desalination capacity, while the US-led coalition bombed Baghdad's water system. From Angola to East Timor, enemies have been killed and their bodies thrown in wells to poison local water supplies.

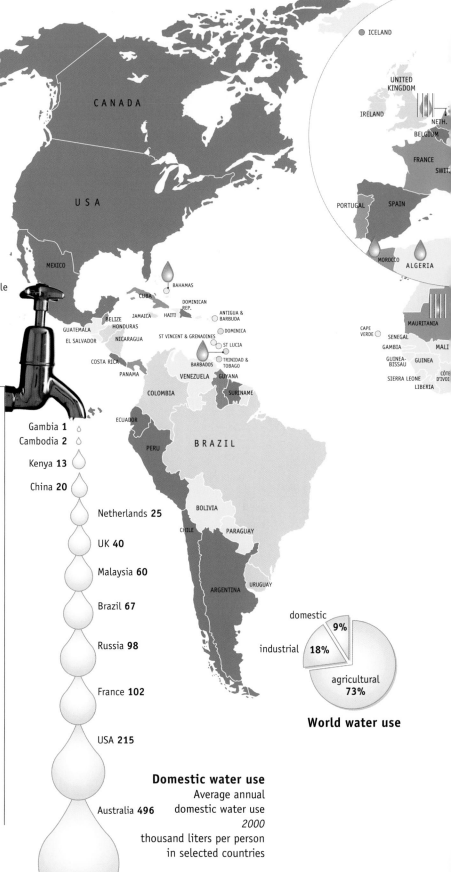

Gambia **1**
Cambodia **2**
Kenya **13**
China **20**
Netherlands **25**
UK **40**
Malaysia **60**
Brazil **67**
Russia **98**
France **102**
USA **215**
Australia **496**

Domestic water use
Average annual
domestic water use
2000
thousand liters per person
in selected countries

domestic **9%**
industrial **18%**
agricultural **73%**

World water use

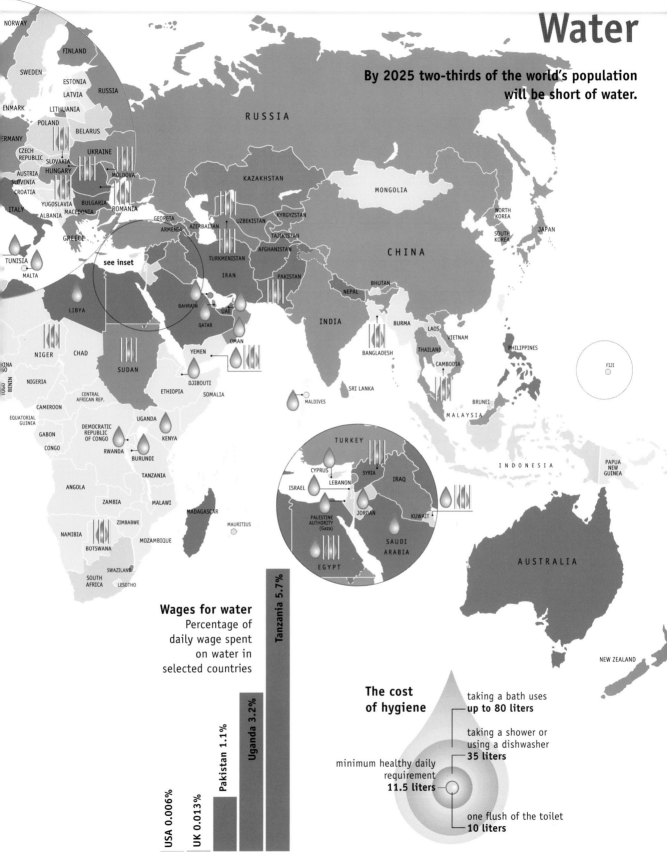

Water

By 2025 two-thirds of the world's population will be short of water.

IT IS SAID THAT the two most commonly used expressions in today's world are "Coca Cola" and "OK". The prominence of one is a triumph of marketing, while the other is used all the time because American culture is so pervasive. Both are in some ways signs of the increasingly global culture in which we live, itself the product of economic globalization. As a result, you can hardly get away from McDonalds even if you want to, you can get cash out of an ATM in more countries than it is worth counting, the same credit cards can be used all over, and most countries' most popular movies are mostly American. So many places have so much that is familiar from so many others that you can get the feeling we are living in a global village.

The more that consumers everywhere have the same wishes and tastes, the more efficiently the global marketplace functions. But globalization and the homogeneity it brings with it are by no means all encompassing and do not sweep all differences aside.

It would be wrong to see these differences as mere remnants from a pre-modern period and on their way out. This is not a matter of the difference of one individual from another, but of social difference – disparities between social groups. Differences of class, wealth and opportunity continue to be the basis

Over 20,000 languages and dialects are spoken worldwide

of conflicting views about how societies should be organized, even if it seems in some countries that the major ideological disputes are less politically important than they once were. Ethnic and religious differences are closely linked to patterns of discrimination, inter-group rivalry, hatred and civil war.

Difference, it seems, can be dangerous, and should be minimized. For example, the great gaps between rich and poor are not only the source, but often the product, of gross injustice, and a program for social peace and justice must include narrowing the gaps. Other differences, however, can be accepted, tolerated and even welcomed.

There have been centuries of religious warfare, racial discrimination and clashes between groups divided and mobilized for conflict along ethno-national lines. It is hard to argue against the proposition that such differences seem at the least to have a tendency to stoke conflict. But from another perspective, it is hard to understand why.

The proposition that my belief is threatened because you believe something else is not tenable. My belief is only threatened if you do something to threaten it, which normally means doing something that threatens me personally or my co-believers. If nobody starts the trouble, we could do as our beliefs command us in perfect peace. Likewise, our differences of pigmentation, language, music, cuisine and other markers of racial and ethno-national identity are in themselves no more threatening than the differences of looks, accent, education and preference to be found among the members of any one identity group.

The potential for violent conflict does not arise from difference alone. It exists when our beliefs command us to do something aggressive to another group – like take their land because we believe our deity promised it to us – and when our own group identity involves identifying another group as an enemy and taking action against them. On a world scale and in a long view, there is more co-existence than violent conflict between different identity groups. And when conflict arises it is usually to do with a battle for power, in which political elites mobilize followers and fighters on ethnic or religious lines. The problem is that once such conflicts have arisen, and the competitive drive for power has dressed itself up in ethnic clothes, it seems particularly difficult to get beyond the hatred and the resentment and move towards reconciliation, even when peace comes.

When national societies are able to avoid the political exploitation of differences of race, religion and ethnicity, they normally find that these differences are a source of strength and richness. The variety of cultures living alongside each other, instead of being a problem and a source of fear, becomes something to take benefit from and to enjoy.

Relative human development
2000 index

The Human Development Index (HDI)
is based on three key components:
longevity, education and income

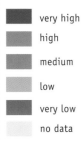

- very high
- high
- medium
- low
- very low
- no data

Income compared with quality of life
Countries that provide a significantly
lower or higher quality of life than their
economic wealth suggests
2000
difference between GDP rank
and HDI rank

- ○ higher quality of life
- ◔ lower quality of life

To the extent that quality of life
can be measured, richer countries
offer more than poor ones.
Whether they do as much as they
are able depends on choices made
about how to allocate their
wealth, especially in making
health care and education
available to all as a right rather
than as a privilege of wealth.

Some countries are ranked much
lower on the UN Human
Development Index than their
economic wealth suggests they
should be. People in these
countries are likely to experience
particularly severe social
inequalities.

**Top-ranked Norway:
GDP per person $30,000
Lowest-ranked
Sierra Leone:
GDP per person $490**

Quality of Life

Quality of life is measured not just by wealth, but also by health and education.

Ups and downs
Countries that have gained or dropped
by 5 or more ranks
on the Human Development Index
1975–2000

⬤ gain in rank since 1975

⬤ drop in rank since 1975

Largest gain: Malaysia, up 14 ranks
Largest drop: El Salvador, down 17 ranks

43

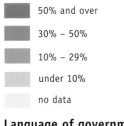

Economic globalization is
changing the way we live so that
we have much more in common
with one another. Television,
films, fashions, fast food, music
and consumer technologies are
the most obvious markers of
growing homogeneity. But deep
differences do survive, and
languages, local culture and
ethnic and national identity are
particularly resilient.

Ethnic difference is often seen
as a problem: both majorities and
minorities often believe another
group threatens their way of life.
Ethnic difference has exploded
into war with extreme violence,
such as the ethnic cleansing of
the Balkan wars in the mid-1990s
and the genocide in Rwanda in
1994.

Acceptance of ethnic diversity,
and mutual tolerance, have
proved to be a more successful
model for peaceful and
prosperous social development
than the exclusion of, and
discrimination against, groups on
grounds of ethnicity, race or
nation. Different ethnic groups
live alongside each other in peace
more than they go to war with
each other.

Ethnicity

Ethnic difference is a source of strength in some societies, and of danger in others.

NORWAY
FINLAND
SWEDEN
ESTONIA
LATVIA
RUSSIA
LITHUANIA
DENMARK
BELARUS
GERMANY
POLAND
CZECH REPUBLIC
SLOVAKIA
UKRAINE
IECH.
AUSTRIA
HUNGARY
SLOVENIA
ROMANIA
MOLDOVA
CROATIA
MARINO
B-H
BULGARIA
ITALY
YUGOSLAVIA
MACEDONIA
ALBANIA
GREECE

RUSSIA

KAZAKHSTAN

MONGOLIA

NORTH KOREA
JAPAN
SOUTH KOREA

TUNISIA
MALTA
GEORGIA
TURKEY
AZERBAIJAN
UZBEKISTAN
KYRGYZSTAN
TURKMENISTAN
TAJIKISTAN
CYPRUS
SYRIA
LEB
ARMENIA
AFGHANISTAN
ISRAEL
IRAQ
IRAN
JORDAN
KUWAIT
PAKISTAN

CHINA

ALGERIA
LIBYA
EGYPT
SAUDI ARABIA
QATAR
BAHRAIN
UAE
NEPAL
BHUTAN
INDIA
BURMA
TAIWAN
Hong Kong

OMAN
YEMEN
DJIBOUTI
ERITREA
LAOS
VIETNAM

MALI
NIGER
CHAD
SUDAN
SOMALIA
THAILAND
CAMBODIA
PHILIPPINES

NIGERIA
CENTRAL AFRICAN REP.
ETHIOPIA
BANGLADESH

CAMEROON
UGANDA
KENYA
SRI LANKA

EQUATORIAL GUINEA
GABON
CONGO
DEMOCRATIC REPUBLIC OF CONGO
RWANDA
SEYCHELLES
SINGAPORE
MALAYSIA
BRUNEI

SÃO TOMÉ & PRÍNCIPE
ANGOLA
BURUNDI
TANZANIA
COMOROS
INDONESIA
EAST TIMOR

ZAMBIA
MALAWI
MADAGASCAR
MAURITIUS

NAMIBIA
ZIMBABWE
BOTSWANA
MOZAMBIQUE

SWAZILAND
SOUTH AFRICA
LESOTHO

MARSHALL ISLANDS
KIRIBATI
TUVALU
WESTERN SAMOA
VANUATU
FRENCH POLYNESIA
NEW CALEDONIA (Fr)
FIJI
TONGA
MICRONESIA
NAURU

PAPUA NEW GUINEA
SOLOMON ISLANDS

AUSTRALIA

NEW ZEALAND

Ethnic and national differences have been at stake in about 45% of civil wars in the current era

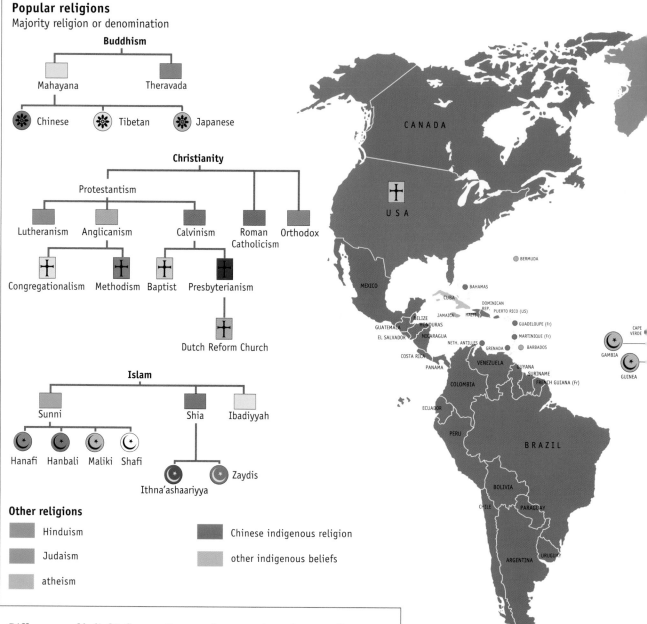

Popular religions

Majority religion or denomination

Buddhism

Mahayana — Theravada

Mahayana:
- ✳ Chinese
- ✳ Tibetan
- ✳ Japanese

Christianity

Protestantism — Roman Catholicism — Orthodox

Protestantism:
- Lutheranism
- Anglicanism
- Calvinism

Anglicanism:
- Congregationalism
- Methodism

Calvinism:
- Baptist
- Presbyterianism

Presbyterianism:
- Dutch Reform Church

Islam

Sunni — Shia — Ibadiyyah

Sunni:
- ☪ Hanafi
- ☪ Hanbali
- ☪ Maliki
- ☪ Shafi

Shia:
- ☪ Ithna'ashaariyya
- ☪ Zaydis

Other religions

- Hinduism
- Judaism
- atheism
- Chinese indigenous religion
- other indigenous beliefs

CANADA

U S A

BERMUDA

MEXICO

BAHAMAS

CUBA

DOMINICAN REP.

PUERTO RICO (US)

BELIZE

JAMAICA

HAITI

GUADELOUPE (Fr)

GUATEMALA

HONDURAS

MARTINIQUE (Fr)

EL SALVADOR

NICARAGUA

NETH. ANTILLES

GRENADA

BARBADOS

COSTA RICA

PANAMA

VENEZUELA

GUYANA

SURINAME

FRENCH GUIANA (Fr)

COLOMBIA

ECUADOR

PERU

BRAZIL

BOLIVIA

CHILE

PARAGUAY

ARGENTINA

URUGUAY

CAPE VERDE

GAMBIA

GUINEA

Differences of belief influence the different ways in which people think, how they behave and what they expect from life. They are among the deepest cultural differences.

The impressive statistics for the number said to belong to one religion or another mask the many schisms within the major religions. Differences within religions – between Sunni and Shia Muslims, for example, or between Protestant and Catholic Christians – are often as intensely felt and argued about as differences between them.

The numbers also hide the difference between practising believers and those who merely claim adherence to a faith but do little to express it. In western Europe, for example, far more people profess a faith than practice it.

Beliefs

The world's largest religions are Christianity (about 2 billion believers) and Islam (just over 1 billion).

see inset

80% of the world's population profess a religious belief, but far fewer practice their religion

Disparities

Distribution of wealth
within a country
1990s
Gini index

The Gini formulation is a widely used way
of calculating inequality within countries.
It measures the degree to which the
distribution of wealth within an economy
is different from a perfectly equal
distribution. The more the inequality,
the higher the index.

	60 and over	*least equal*
	50 – 59	
	40 – 49	
	30 – 39	
	20 – 29	*most equal*
	no data	

Disparities of wealth within
countries are in every way as
important as disparities between
them. The average GDP per
person, used to measure the
wealth of a country, masks the
internal differences – such as the
disparity between rich and poor
regions, between social classes,
and between men and women, as
well as the poverty of particular
ethnic, national or racial groups.

With wealth comes power, and
therefore the ability to get more
wealth, and thus more power.
And with poverty comes a self-
reinforcing spiral in the opposite
direction. The Gini index thus
offers a rough indication about
inequalities of power as well
as wealth.

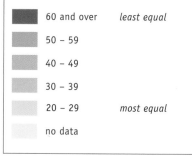

**45 million people
in the USA
are living in poverty**

Rich and Poor

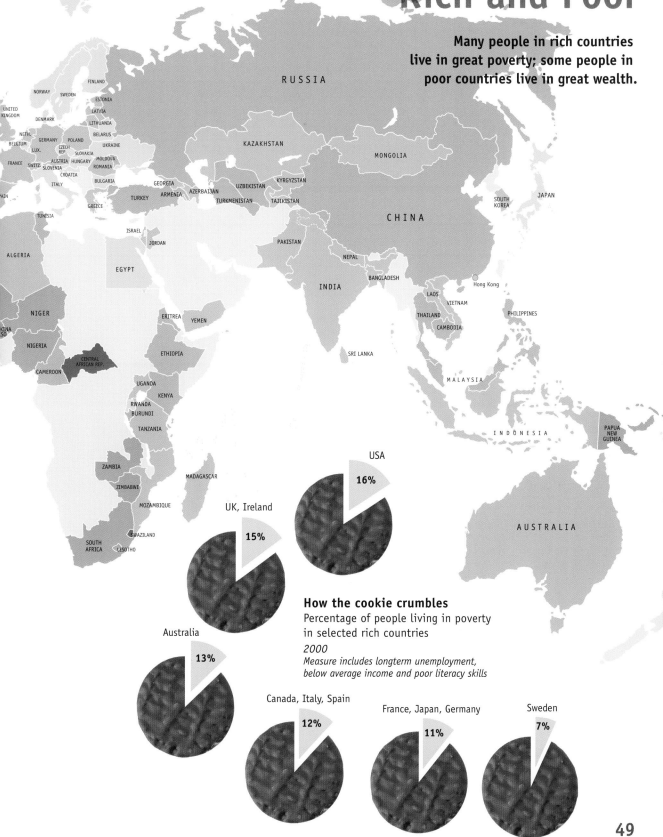

Many people in rich countries live in great poverty; some people in poor countries live in great wealth.

USA
16%

UK, Ireland
15%

Australia
13%

How the cookie crumbles
Percentage of people living in poverty in selected rich countries

2000
Measure includes longterm unemployment, below average income and poor literacy skills

Canada, Italy, Spain
12%

France, Japan, Germany
11%

Sweden
7%

70% and over

50% – 69%

30% – 59%

10% – 29%

under 10%

no data

over 70% of illiterate adults
are women

more illiterate adults are men
than women

Illiteracy is still widespread in many countries, and in almost all there are more illiterate women than men. In some, women make up 70 percent or more of the illiterate population, reducing their opportunities for economic and social independence.

Literacy is a requirement for people to function in modern societies, and is likewise a requirement for modern societies to be able to function. Better educated workforces tend to be more productive. Literacy also brings rich benefits – broader horizons and the possibility of greater knowledge and understanding, along with new sources of entertainment. There is still a substantial minority of people, though, who are functionally illiterate – lacking sufficient skills to play a full part in society.

Two-thirds of illiterate adults are women

Functional illiteracy
Percentage of adults
unable to read and write well enough
to function effectively in the community
2000
selected industrialized countries

Portugal 48%
Poland 43%
UK 22%
USA 21%
Australia 17%
Germany 14%
Sweden 8%

Literacy

Although more people are learning to read and write than ever before, there are still 860 million illiterate adults worldwide.

ICELAND
NORWAY
SWEDEN
FINLAND
UNITED KINGDOM
IRELAND
DENMARK
ESTONIA
RUSSIA
LATVIA
LITHUANIA
NETH.
GERMANY
POLAND
BELARUS
BELGIUM
LUX.
CZECH REPUBLIC
SLOVAKIA
UKRAINE
FRANCE
SWITZ.
AUSTRIA
HUNGARY
MOLDOVA
SLOVENIA
ROMANIA
CROATIA
YUGOSLAVIA
BULGARIA
PORTUGAL
ITALY
ALBANIA
SPAIN
GREECE
MALTA
AZERBAIJAN
ARMENIA
TURKMENISTAN
UZBEKISTAN
KYRGYZSTAN
TAJIKISTAN

RUSSIA
KAZAKHSTAN
MONGOLIA
JAPAN
CHINA
SOUTH KOREA

see inset
IRAN
BAHRAIN
QATAR
UAE
OMAN
YEMEN
PAKISTAN
NEPAL
INDIA
BANGLADESH
BURMA
LAOS
VIETNAM
THAILAND
CAMBODIA
Hong Kong
BRUNEI
SINGAPORE
MALAYSIA
PHILIPPINES
SAMOA
FIJI

MOROCCO
ALGERIA
LIBYA
TUNISIA
MALI
NIGER
CHAD
SUDAN
ERITREA
DJIBOUTI
ETHIOPIA
SOMALIA
BURKINA FASO
NIGERIA
GHANA
TOGO
BENIN
CÔTE D'IVOIRE
CAMEROON
EQUATORIAL GUINEA
CAMEROON
CONGO
CENTRAL AFRICAN REP.
DEMOCRATIC REPUBLIC OF CONGO
UGANDA
RWANDA
BURUNDI
KENYA
TANZANIA
COMOROS
ANGOLA
ZAMBIA
MALAWI
MADAGASCAR
MAURITIUS
REUNION
NAMIBIA
ZIMBABWE
MOZAMBIQUE
BOTSWANA
SWAZILAND
SOUTH AFRICA
LESOTHO
MALDIVES
SRI LANKA

TURKEY
CYPRUS
SYRIA
LEBANON
ISRAEL
JORDAN
KUWAIT
EGYPT
SAUDI ARABIA

INDONESIA
PAPUA NEW GUINEA
AUSTRALIA
NEW ZEALAND

Primary school enrolment

Percentage of children of primary-school age who enrol in school
2000
selected regions

| Sub-Saharan Africa 60% | South Asia 71% | Middle East and North Africa 81% | Latin America and Caribbean 91% | Central and Eastern Europe, CIS and Baltic States 87% | East Asia and Pacific 95% |

The industrial revolution of the 18th and 19th centuries took people off the land and into the cities – off the farms and into factories. As economic development has continued, the majority of jobs have moved from the manufacturing industries and into the service sector, including the information business.

The pattern of world employment shows an economic gulf between countries where the service sector predominates, and those that are two stages behind, with most of their employment still in agriculture. Some of these countries, however, including the most populous ones in Asia, are now developing large service sectors themselves.

In all sectors, the work of people is reinforced and often replaced by machines. Robotics and computerization mean that fewer workers can carry out more tasks.

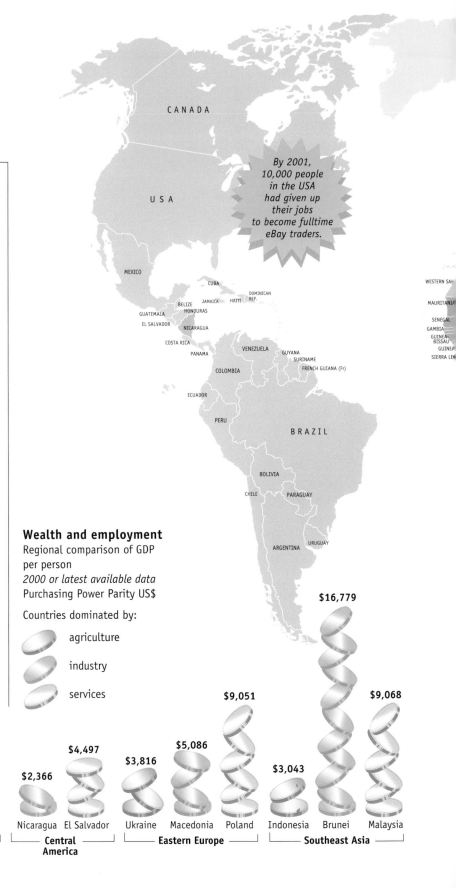

By 2001, 10,000 people in the USA had given up their jobs to become fulltime eBay traders.

Wealth and employment
Regional comparison of GDP per person
2000 or latest available data
Purchasing Power Parity US$

Countries dominated by:

agriculture

industry

services

$16,779

$9,051

$9,068

$4,497

$3,816

$5,086

$3,043

$2,366

$523

$746

$1,022

Tanzania	Niger	Kenya	Nicaragua	El Salvador	Ukraine	Macedonia	Poland	Indonesia	Brunei	Malaysia

Africa — **Central America** — **Eastern Europe** — **Southeast Asia**

Workplaces

Economic development and increasing national prosperity mark a shift from agriculture to industry and from industry to the service sector.

Working hours
Average number of hours
worked each year
2000 or latest available
selected industrialized countries

- Norway 1,376
- Germany 1,480
- France 1,604
- Italy 1,682
- Brazil 1,689
- UK 1,719
- Pakistan 1,723
- Japan 1,842
- Australia 1,860
- Mexico 1,887
- USA 1,978
- Portugal 2,009
- Peru 2,091
- Czech Republic 2,092
- Malaysia 2,244
- Bangladesh 2,301
- South Korea 2,474

The hours worked by an average US worker are 25% more productive than those of a worker in the UK.

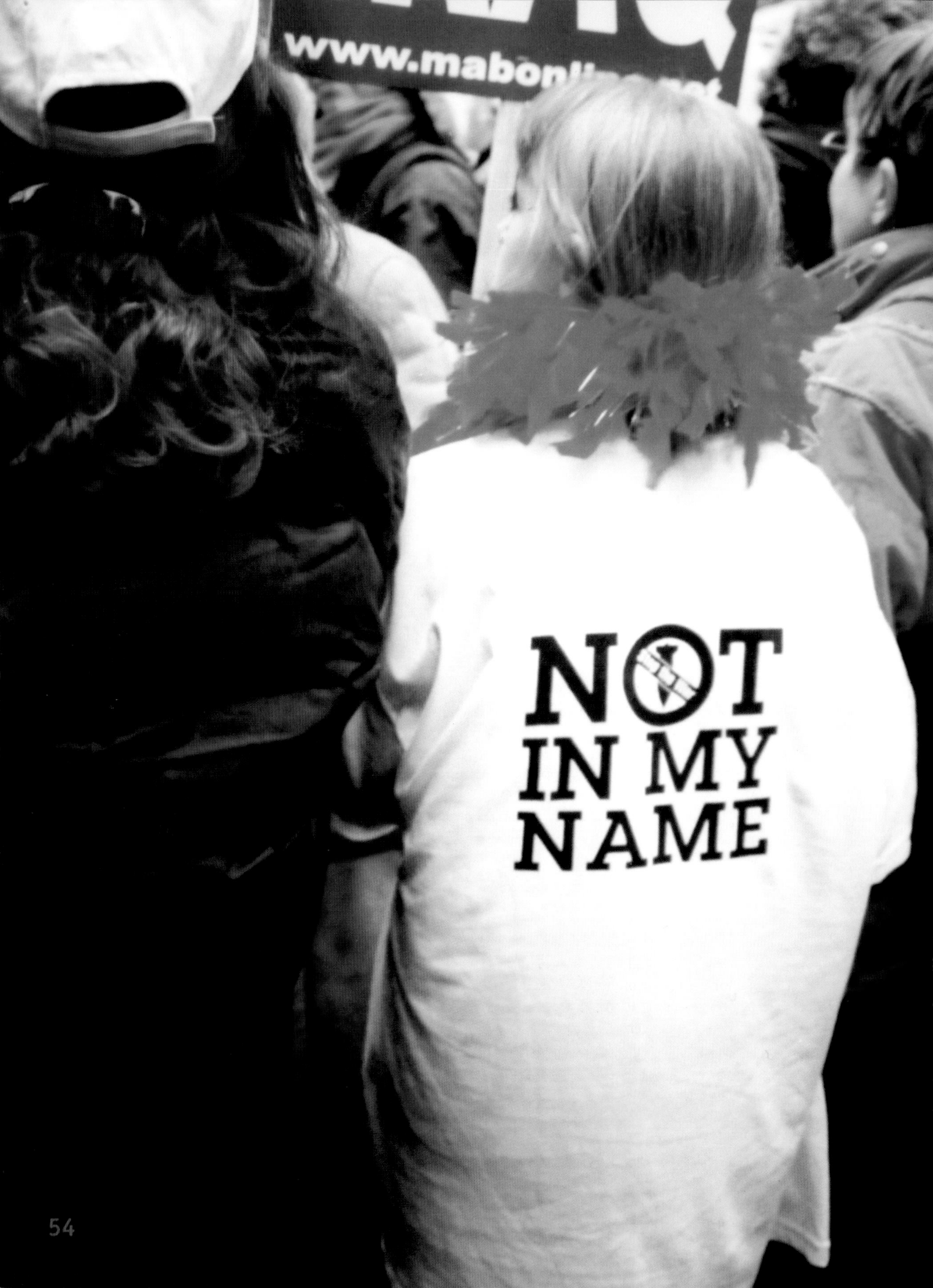
www.mabonl
NOT
IN MY
NAME

ONE CHARACTERISTIC OF MODERNITY is its emphasis on the rights and freedoms of the individual. This emphasis emerged in post-Renaissance Europe in political philosophy, and began to inform political practice in the American War of Independence and the French Revolution, in the last three decades of the 18th century. Today, human rights are major components of our discourse about society and politics.

That does not mean that human rights are respected all the time. They are attacked and restricted because those with power know that a world in which rights are fully respected is a world where power is much more limited.

For the most part, denials and abuses of human rights are not accompanied by a justification. But there are three arguments that are sometimes used to justify restrictions and attacks on rights and freedom.

The first is the argument that group rights should take precedence over individual rights. This is sometimes expressed by political leaders in Asia and the Middle East as a rejection of the western cult of individualism in favor of a more collective worldview. A different version of the same argument is heard in the west when national security is made a reason for curtailing individual liberties. It is an argument based on the greater good of the larger group.

There is much that is valid in this argument, for an individual cannot be more important than the group to which she or he belongs. On the other hand, if the rights of individuals are trampled or denied in the name of a group, one wonders what the group is for. If a state does not protect its people, each of whom is an individual, it undermines its own legitimacy. And, all too often, the argument of the greater good is made by a leader trying to find a moral defense for his or her own excessive power.

The second reservation about the discourse of human rights is that it is wrong to treat everybody equally because people are not equal, and too much emphasis on equality means treating them as if they are uniform. This argument has been highly influential in, for example, resisting racial equality and equal rights and opportunities for women – influential, maybe, but shallow. Equality and uniformity are not the same idea. Equality is about the law, and says we should all be treated equally; the facts of your social class, gender, belief, race, nationality or sexual preference should no more determine how you are treated by the law than should your shoe size. Uniformity is about being the same as everybody else, and, given how different we are from each other, it would be an abuse of our rights and lead to unequal treatment to try to force us to be the same.

The third reservation about the emphasis on human rights is that it leads to forgetting that individuals have responsibilities towards each other, and therefore towards the larger group of which they are a member. Normally, the way in which individual rights are discussed answers one part of this criticism, because the rights we have do not and, speaking philosophically, cannot include doing harm to others by abusing or denying their rights. This is one way in which the arguments about individual rights and group rights can be matched up together.

Another part of the responsibility argument is, though, more important. The reason for emphasizing rights can be thought of as defensive – so that nobody gets bad treatment. The reason for emphasizing responsibility is more outgoing – so that people look after each other. The discourse of human rights can shade too easily into an over-emphasis on the individual as a passive recipient of the benefits of his or her rights. It is not the intention at all of rights advocates, but their discourse sometimes hints at an idea of society in which we each sit there, interested in society and community only for what it can give us as individuals, whining on about rights whenever we get less than we think we deserve. We get a much better and more supportive image of society and community if, alongside respect for rights, we emphasize our responsibilities to look after each other. This is the sort of sense of responsibility that is expressed by individuals engaging in voluntary activities that care for or help other people, in their own country or abroad – the sense of social responsibility displayed by human rights activists, for example. And by getting a workable balance between rights and responsibilities, we also put an end to the idea that group rights and individual rights must conflict.

Three juveniles are known to have been executed in 2002 – all in Texas, USA

Extreme abuse of human rights
1998–2000

States whose reported abuses
of human rights include:

- extra-judicial executions
- torture
- arbitrary arrest and detention
- mistreatment by police and/or prison authorities
- violent and/or abusive treatment of refugees, asylum seekers and/or immigrants
- other states

The worse the human rights situation, the less possible it is to report all or even most abuses.

The most common kinds of extra-judicial execution are the targeted assassination of political opponents, the murder of prisoners of war, and the systematic elimination of people regarded as socially undesirable, such as criminals for whom the police and justice system have no resources, and street children with no family. Non-governmental activities, such as physical violence by drug cartels, insurgent armies and privately organized vigilante groups, have been excluded, even though they often constitute an abuse of human rights as systematic as anything the state perpetrates.

Each category of abuse in the main map implies that the next one down is also perpetrated; a state that sanctions extra-judicial executions can also be expected to use torture, arbitrary arrest, and random official violence.

In wartime, the first instinct of most governements is to clamp down on rights and freedoms. In some cases the clampdown becomes extreme. Abuse of human rights is both cause and consequence of war.

In 1991
the UN Security Council
established "safe havens"
for Iraqi Kurds;
for the first time,
the right of a sovereign
state to massacre
its own citizens
was denied.

Executions in 2001
selected countries

- **66** USA
- **79** Saudi Arabia
- **139** Iran
- **2,468** China

Human Rights

The abuse of human rights is more visible, and global awareness of it more focused, but there is no evidence that even the most extreme abuses are declining.

SWEDEN
UNITED KINGDOM
BELGIUM
GERMANY
POLAND
LITHUANIA
BELARUS
FRANCE
CZECH REP.
SK
UKRAINE
SWITZ
AUSTRIA
HUNGARY
MOLDOVA
SLOVENIA
CROATIA
B-H
YUG
ROMANIA
ITALY
BULGARIA
ALBANIA
MACEDONIA
GREECE

RUSSIA

KAZAKHSTAN

GEORGIA
ARMENIA
AZERBAIJAN
UZBEKISTAN
KYRGYZSTAN
TURKMENISTAN
TAJIKISTAN

MONGOLIA

JAPAN
SOUTH KOREA

TUNISIA
LIBYA
ALGERIA
see inset
IRAN
AFGHANISTAN
PAKISTAN
CHINA

BAHRAIN
QATAR
UAE
SAUDI ARABIA

NEPAL
BHUTAN
INDIA
BANGLADESH
BURMA
LAOS

TAIWAN

NIGER
CHAD
SUDAN
ERITREA
YEMEN
DJIBOUTI
F
BENIN
TOGO
NIGERIA
CAMEROON
CENTRAL AFRICAN REP.
ETHIOPIA
SOMALIA
EQUATORIAL GUINEA
UGANDA
KENYA
CONGO
DEMOCRATIC REPUBLIC OF CONGO
RWANDA
BURUNDI
TANZANIA

VIETNAM
THAILAND
CAMBODIA
PHILIPPINES

MALDIVES
SRI LANKA

BRUNEI
MALAYSIA
SINGAPORE

SAMOA
VANUATU
FIJI

ANGOLA
ZAMBIA
MALAWI
NAMIBIA
ZIMBABWE
MOZAMBIQUE
SWAZILAND
SOUTH AFRICA
LESOTHO

MAURITIUS

I N D O N E S I A

PAPUA NEW GUINEA
SOLOMON ISLANDS

TURKEY
CYPRUS
LEBANON
SYRIA
PALESTINIAN AUTHORITY
ISRAEL
JORDAN
IRAQ
KUWAIT
EGYPT
SAUDI ARABIA

AUSTRALIA

ANTIGUA & BARBUDA
ST KITTS & NEVIS
DOMINICA
ST LUCIA
BARBADOS
ST VINCENT & GRENADINES
TRINIDAD & TOBAGO
BAHAMAS
CUBA
JAMAICA

BAHRAIN

SINGAPORE

COMOROS

Judicial killing

Countries that retain the death penalty
late 1999

● capital punishment is legal

○ other countries

Freedom of the press
2001

The Freedom House survey of press freedom used here defines press freedom in terms of official (i.e. government) censorship, interference and influence in the delivery of news to the people; the role of private owners of news organisations is not included.

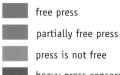

- free press
- partially free press
- press is not free
- heavy press censorship
- no data

A dangerous profession

 journalists have been killed because of their professional activities

journalists have been physically attacked – or allowed to be attacked – by state officials

journalists and/or other media professionals have been imprisoned for their professional activities

Freedom of the press and news media has long been regarded as an essential element of a free society. Nowhere is the press perfectly free, and arguably nor should it be: most liberal societies agree some restrictions are justified, such as on hate speech. It is when the media are restricted from carrying information and opinion critical of government and state that citizens' freedom is at risk.

In many countries, legal, administrative and economic measures to shackle the press are backed by attacks on journalists and other media professionals. Sometimes servants of the state carry out the attacks. Sometimes, by watching or by not investigating the crime, they tacitly but unmistakeably condone the attacks. In countries as diverse as Colombia, Spain and the UK, journalists' lives are also sometimes at risk from criminals and extremists.

Only 20% of the world's population have access to free press

ICELAND

CANADA

USA

MEXICO

BAHAMAS

CUBA

DOMINICAN REP.

HAITI

JAMAICA

BELIZE

GUATEMALA

HONDURAS

EL SALVADOR

NICARAGUA

COSTA RICA

PANAMA

ANTIGUA & BARBUDA

ST KITTS & NEVIS

DOMINICA

ST VINCENT & GRENAD.

ST LUCIA

GRENADA

BARBADOS

TRINIDAD & TOBAGO

VENEZUELA

GUYANA

SURINAME

COLOMBIA

ECUADOR

PERU

BRAZIL

BOLIVIA

PARAGUAY

CHILE

ARGENTINA

URUGUAY

UNITED KINGDOM

IRELAND

NETH.

BELGIUM

LUX.

FRANCE

SWITZ.

PORTUGAL

SPAIN

MOROCCO

ALGERIA

CAPE VERDE

MAURITANIA

SENEGAL

MALI

GAMBIA

GUINEA-BISSAU

GUINEA

SIERRA LEONE

CÔTE D'IVOIRE

LIBERIA

Free Speech

Article 19 of the Universal Declaration of Human Rights states that everyone has the right to freedom of opinion and expression, including the right to receive and to communicate information and ideas.

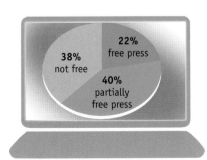

Press freedom
Percentage of people living under different degrees of press freedom

Total population in countries surveyed: 6,096 billion

22% free press
38% not free
40% partially free press

Almost 250 million people below the age of 17 are working; almost half of them are doing jobs that are unsuitable for their age, and no fewer than 179 million of them are caught in the worst forms of child labor, such as slavery, prostitution and forced recruitment for armed forces.

Child soldiers live in a world of unremitting brutality. Recruitment is often accomplished by physical and psychological coercion. There are well-documented cases of children being recruited on the credible threat of otherwise losing a limb. Once recruited, they are often blooded by having to perform a cruel act – such as killing their parents or an unwilling recruit. Many are sexually abused. They face extreme punishments. And to keep them compliant, not only do they face extreme punishments, but large numbers live in a semi-stupor from the drugs and alcohol provided by their commanders.

If peace breaks out, helping child soldiers find a normal life is a major problem. They have lost their homes, upbringing, education and moral sense. It is no surprise if they turn to crime.

CANADA

USA

MEXICO

CUBA

JAMAICA   HAITI

EL SALVADOR   NICARAGUA   ANTIGUA & BARBUDA

GRENADA   BARBADOS

VENEZUELA   TRINIDAD & TOBAGO

COLOMBIA   SURINAME

PERU   BRAZIL

BOLIVIA

PARAGUAY

IREI

MAURITANIA

GUINEA-BISSAU

GUINEA

CÔ
D'IVO

SIERRA LEONE

LIBERIA

Over 300,000 people below the age of 18 are fighting in wars

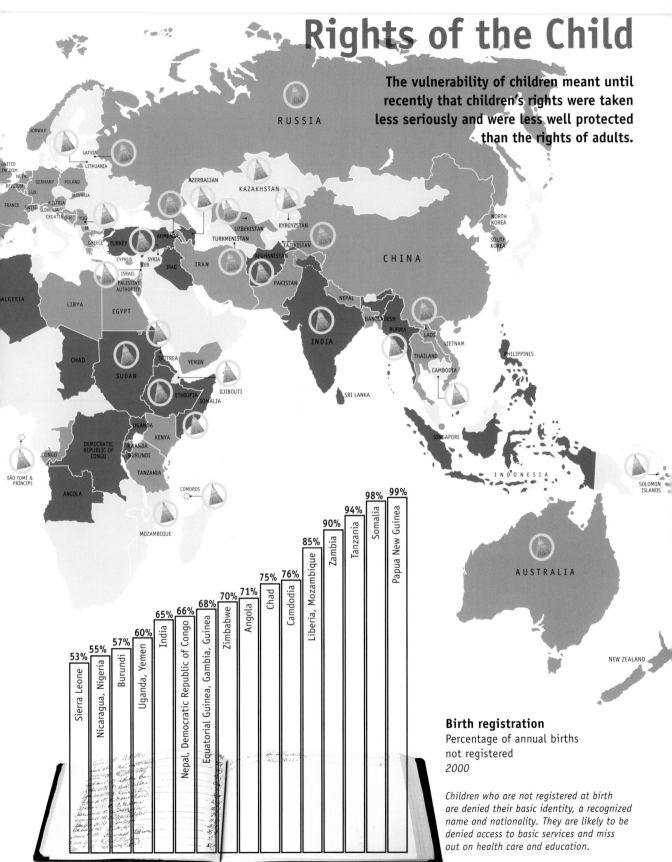

Rights of the Child

The vulnerability of children meant until recently that children's rights were taken less seriously and were less well protected than the rights of adults.

Birth registration
Percentage of annual births
not registered
2000

Children who are not registered at birth are denied their basic identity, a recognized name and nationality. They are likely to be denied access to basic services and miss out on health care and education.

Country	%
Sierra Leone	53%
Nicaragua, Nigeria	55%
Burundi	57%
Uganda, Yemen	60%
India	65%
Nepal, Democratic Republic of Congo	66%
Equatorial Guinea, Gambia, Guinea	68%
Zimbabwe	70%
Angola	71%
Chad	75%
Camdodia	76%
Liberia, Mozambique	85%
Zambia	90%
Tanzania	94%
Somalia	98%
Papua New Guinea	99%

Some people, some parties and some governments maintain that only a narrow range of sexual activity should be allowed. As well as banning same-sex relationships, there have been attempts to ban specific activities and allow others only on certain days of the week.

In some countries, there is legal tolerance of different sexual choices but plenty of discrimination in practice; in others, intolerant laws are seldom applied. But almost everywhere, those whose sexual preference takes them outside the norm – and especially gay men – face pressures that are subtle and social when they are not open and political.

The most extreme form of sexual policing is the tacit acceptance in some countries of the murder of women or girls who are raped, or whose behavior is considered sexually inappropriate. The killing is usually done by a man from the same family, in the name of the family's honor.

In almost all countries, sexual activity is more widespread than the moral guardians acknowledge. When condoms are expensive, the costs of sexual freedom can be very high.

Burma
Burundi

Ethiopia
Togo

CAR
Madagascar
Mali

Guinea
Rwanda
Congo
Benin
Laos

France
Japan
Singapore
UK
USA

Cost of condoms
Cost of one year's supply
as a proportion of
GNP per person
1990s

less than 1%   10%–16%   23%–27%   30%–31%   42%–45%

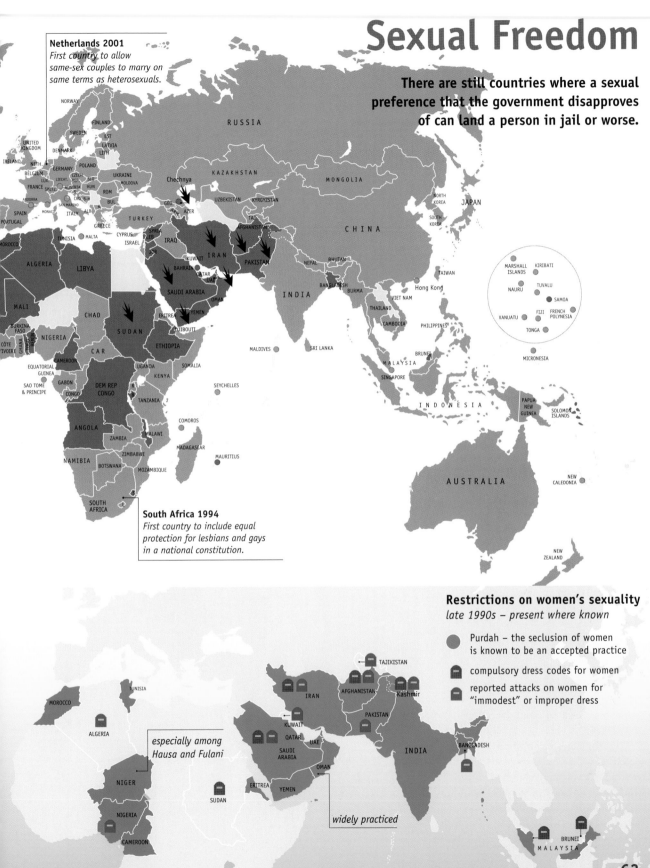

Sexual Freedom

There are still countries where a sexual preference that the government disapproves of can land a person in jail or worse.

Netherlands 2001
First country to allow same-sex couples to marry on same terms as heterosexuals.

South Africa 1994
First country to include equal protection for lesbians and gays in a national constitution.

Restrictions on women's sexuality
late 1990s – present where known

- Purdah – the seclusion of women is known to be an accepted practice
- compulsory dress codes for women
- reported attacks on women for "immodest" or improper dress

especially among Hausa and Fulani

widely practiced

63

Freedom and restriction

State attitudes to the religion of the majority and other religions
1999

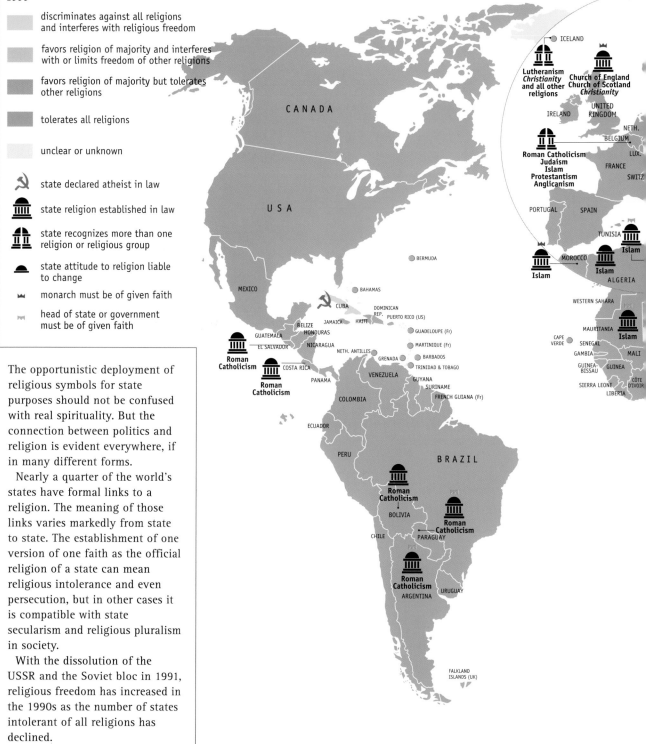

- discriminates against all religions and interferes with religious freedom
- favors religion of majority and interferes with or limits freedom of other religions
- favors religion of majority but tolerates other religions
- tolerates all religions
- unclear or unknown

- state declared atheist in law
- state religion established in law
- state recognizes more than one religion or religious group
- state attitude to religion liable to change
- monarch must be of given faith
- head of state or government must be of given faith

The opportunistic deployment of religious symbols for state purposes should not be confused with real spirituality. But the connection between politics and religion is evident everywhere, if in many different forms.

Nearly a quarter of the world's states have formal links to a religion. The meaning of those links varies markedly from state to state. The establishment of one version of one faith as the official religion of a state can mean religious intolerance and even persecution, but in other cases it is compatible with state secularism and religious pluralism in society.

With the dissolution of the USSR and the Soviet bloc in 1991, religious freedom has increased in the 1990s as the number of states intolerant of all religions has declined.

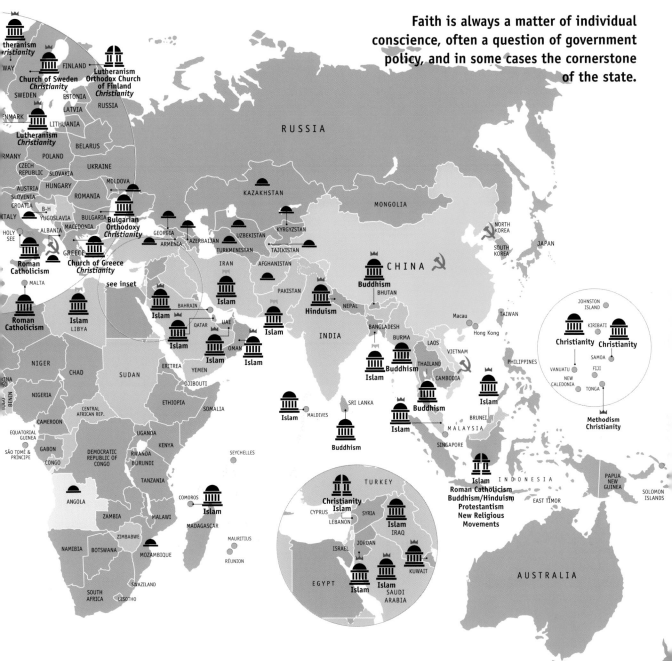

Religious Freedom

Faith is always a matter of individual conscience, often a question of government policy, and in some cases the cornerstone of the state.

theranism
ristianity

WAY

Church of Sweden
Christianity
SWEDEN

FINLAND

Lutheranism
Orthodox Church
of Finland
Christianity
ESTONIA

LATVIA

RUSSIA

NMARK

LITHUANIA

Lutheranism
Christianity

RMANY

BELARUS

POLAND

CZECH
REPUBLIC

SLOVAKIA

UKRAINE

RUSSIA

AUSTRIA

HUNGARY

SLOVENIA

ROMANIA

MOLDOVA

CROATIA

B-H

ITALY

YUGOSLAVIA

BULGARIA

KAZAKHSTAN

MONGOLIA

NORTH
KOREA

JAPAN

HOLY
SEE

ALBANIA

MACEDONIA

Bulgarian
Orthodoxy
Christianity

GEORGIA

SOUTH
KOREA

Roman
Catholicism

GREECE

Church of Greece
Christianity

AZERBAIJAN

ARMENIA

UZBEKISTAN

KYRGYZSTAN

TAJIKISTAN

CHINA

Buddhism

TAIWAN

MALTA

see inset

TURKMENISTAN

IRAN

AFGHANISTAN

BHUTAN

Macau

Roman
Catholicism

Islam
LIBYA

Islam

BAHRAIN

Islam

QATAR

UAE

PAKISTAN

Islam

NEPAL

Hinduism

INDIA

BANGLADESH

BURMA

LAOS

Hong Kong

VIETNAM

PHILIPPINES

JOHNSTON
ISLAND

KIRIBATI

Christianity   Christianity

SAMOA

VANUATU

FIJI

NEW
CALEDONIA

TONGA

Methodism
Christianity

NIGER

CHAD

SUDAN

ERITREA

YEMEN

OMAN

Islam

Islam

THAILAND

Buddhism

CAMBODIA

Islam

BRUNEI

KINA
SO

BENIN

NIGERIA

CENTRAL
AFRICAN REP.

ETHIOPIA

DJIBOUTI

SOMALIA

Islam

MALDIVES

SRI LANKA

Buddhism

MALAYSIA

SINGAPORE

CAMEROON

EQUATORIAL
GUINEA

SÃO TOMÉ &
PRÍNCIPE

GABON

CONGO

DEMOCRATIC
REPUBLIC OF
CONGO

UGANDA

RWANDA

BURUNDI

KENYA

TANZANIA

SEYCHELLES

Buddhism

Islam

INDONESIA

Roman Catholicism
Buddhism/Hinduism
Protestantism
New Religious
Movements

PAPUA
NEW
GUINEA

EAST TIMOR

SOLOMON
ISLANDS

ANGOLA

ZAMBIA

MALAWI

COMOROS

Islam

MADAGASCAR

MAURITIUS

RÉUNION

TURKEY

Christianity
Islam

CYPRUS

LEBANON

SYRIA

Islam
IRAQ

AUSTRALIA

NAMIBIA

ZIMBABWE

BOTSWANA

MOZAMBIQUE

JORDAN

ISRAEL

KUWAIT

SWAZILAND

SOUTH
AFRICA

LESOTHO

EGYPT

Islam

Islam
SAUDI
ARABIA

NEW ZEALAND

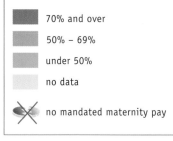
In Europe, Australasia and North America, it is much less common than it used to be for women to be openly referred to as second class citizens. But polite silence on the issue cannot mask the reality that women continue, in general, to be given less well-paid jobs than men, and get paid less than men even when they are doing the same job. Likewise, although women are more present in politics than before, most political leaders are men. And outside Europe, Australasia and North America, women tend to be worse off and more excluded from power.

One of the most sensitive and controversial rights of a woman is to control her own fertility. There are about 50 million abortions a year, of which about 20 million are illegal and so unsafe that about 80,000 women each year die as a result. Emotions on the issue run deep, but the capacity of the law to regulate it satisfactorily is at least questionable. In extreme cases, opponents of abortion rights end up by committing against living people the same crime – murder – as they set out to prevent being committed against the unborn.

There is no country
in the world where:
• women are a majority
of the highest executive
body in government
• women are
a majority
in parliament.

Abortion and the law
2002 or latest available data

illegal or severely restricted only to save woman's life

legal to save life or preserve the health of woman and/or if the fetus is impaired

legal for social or economic reasons

legal on request but usually with gestational limits

Women's Rights

In many countries the relative position of women is improving, but in most countries their position is far worse than men's.

67

Part 5
War and Force

THE USE OF FORCE remains the ultimate arbiter of high-stakes political disputes; the capacity to use it is the most direct – if also the bluntest and least sophisticated – form of power. Although warfare and the maintenance of armed forces are a constant factor of world politics, there have been two epochal changes in the military dimension of international relations in barely more than a decade.

In the last three months of 1989, the Cold War between the USA and the USSR and their respective allies came to an end. There followed a decade in which two contradictory trends vied with each other. Expectations of a more peaceful world turned out to be unjustified. The number of wars each year increased sharply in the early 1990s. On the other hand, there was a peace dividend: military spending fell dramatically, the number of nuclear weapons was cut, and the UN undertook more peace operations than before.

The second change came as a result of the suicide attacks on the World Trade Centre and the Pentagon on September 11, 2001 that killed over 3,000 people of over 80 nationalities. Although the attacks had spectacularly chilling results, it was not the attacks themselves that opened a new era. Rather, it was the American response.

Since the Vietnam War, and the protest it generated within the USA, the general assumption had been that US domestic opinion would not tolerate American deaths in foreign wars of intervention. Accordingly, official US doctrines for the use of military force insisted on quick actions involving overwhelming force, minimal US casualties, and full support from the US public. These conditions could rarely be met. They not only limited the number of US military actions, but, when force was used, they also set the pattern of high-tech, low-risk war. The 1991 Gulf War began with five weeks of heavy bombing. The 1999 war against Yugoslavia was conducted exclusively from the air for eleven weeks.

These inhibitions about the use of force were abandoned in the reaction to 9/11. It was a surprise to many observers that when American forces went to war to overthrow the Taliban in Afghanistan in October 2001, ground forces were quickly involved in limited numbers. Against Iraq in March 2003, the US launched a major ground offensive at the same time as the bombing and missile attacks started. The reaction to 9/11 unleashed American military power, first in central Asia and then in the Middle East.

It had this effect, in part, because 9/11 produced – as its authors meant it to – a sense of being threatened. Such a feeling often induces a willingness to take risks that would otherwise not be acceptable. So 9/11 resulted in strong support within American public opinion for the use of US force abroad. This will last for as long as the sense of insecurity lasts. If that feeling abates, the USA will probably ease down on its international military posture and the accompanying doctrine of pre-emption – a statement of willingness and a claim of the right to retaliate before a possible attack is launched against the US. And, of course, further devastating attacks on American soil or on Americans abroad are likely to lead to attitudes hardening.

One part of the problem with this is that fear is not a particularly good guide to policy-making. In a few months after 9/11, the focus of US policy shifted. It went from the threat from global terrorists, to the possibility that terrorists might get weapons of mass destruction, to a state that had long tried to get hold of such weapons and might still have them. The terrorists who launched 9/11 had no identifiable connection with this state and had offered to fight against it a decade before. But the focus of American policy slid from al Qaida to Iraq with no pause for thought, motored by the administration's grand strategy for the Middle East region, and the winning of public support through the mind-numbing emotion of fear.

The other problem of policy based on this sense of threat is that America's international agenda will be heavily influenced by what others do, and especially by the actions of a small number of criminal international organizations. It is an irony of having such extraordinary power that the USA's actions could end up being indirectly dictated by others with much less power. It is an irony that could have heavy consequences for Americans and for the rest of the world, an irony that could be avoided if US policy set out honestly to address the causes rather than waiting for the symptoms to erupt.

War and the extreme abuse of human rights go hand in hand

Wars since the Cold War
1990–March 2003

- states involved in armed conflict *since 1990*
- other states

Location of wars

- war *2002–2003*
- recent war *since 1990*
- recent tension *since 1990*

The end of the Cold War was the end of an era of international relations. As the USSR and former Yugoslavia broke up, the number of wars each year increased sharply. The international news media started to report the extraordinary cruelty displayed in many of the wars, especially in Bosnia-Herzegovina and Chechnya, and worst of all in Rwanda, where 800,000 people were massacred in a six-week period in 1994.

Under 10 percent of today's wars are between states. The pattern of most civil wars is one of bursts of activity alternating with long periods of relative calm. As a result, most wars stay out of the news media most of the time. Over half of today's civil wars have lasted more than five years; in long-lasting conflicts, it is not just the original causes that keep the war going, but the harm each side has done to the other and the pain and bitterness that result.

The symbols on the map show where wars were being fought in the 1990s and in 2002–3 but do not show how many wars were fought in each country or region.

7 million people have been killed in wars since 1989 – 75% were civilians

States fighting wars outside their borders in 2003 include Australia, UK and USA in Iraq.

Over 15,000 people are killed or injured by landmines and unexploded ordnance each year.

CANADA
USA
MEXICO
CUBA
HAITI
DOMINICAN REP.
GUATEMALA
EL SALVADOR
NICARAGUA
VENEZUELA
COLOMBIA
SURINAME
ECUADOR
PERU

Northern Ireland
UNITED KINGDOM
FRANCE
SPAIN
MOROCCO
ALGERIA
WESTERN SAHARA
MAURITANIA
SENEGAL
MALI
GUINEA-BISSAU
GUINEA
SIERRA LEONE
CÔTE D'IVOIRE
LIBERIA

Anti-personnel mines
Number of mines estimated to be in the arsenals of 94 countries *2002*

Total: 230 million

- other countries **23 million**
- Belarus **4.5 million**
- India **4.5 million**
- Pakistan **6 million**
- Ukraine **6 million**
- USA **11 million**
- China **110 million**
- Russia **65 million**

War

There have been 125 wars worldwide since the end of the Cold War in late 1989.

ORWAY

RUSSIA
Moscow

Ingushetia/
North Ossetia

Chechnya

Dagestan

RUSSIA

Nagorno-
Karabakh

SLOVENIA

MOLDOVA

CROATIA

B-H

YUGOSLAVIA

ALBANIA   MACEDONIA

Sarajevo

GEORGIA

ARMENIA   AZERBAIJAN

UZBEKISTAN

NORTH
KOREA

GREECE

TAJIKISTAN

see inset

AFGHANISTAN

Punjab

CHINA

Assam,
Manipur,
Tripura

IRAN

NEPAL

Nagaland

TAIWAN

LIBYA

PAKISTAN

INDIA

BANGLADESH

BURMA

LAOS

Andra Pradesh

NIGER

CHAD

SUDAN

ERITREA

YEMEN

DJIBOUTI

SOMALIA

PHILIPPINES

Spratly
Islands

NIGERIA

CENTRAL
AFRICAN REP.

ETHIOPIA

SRI LANKA

CAMBODIA

Phnom Penh

CONGO

UGANDA

RWANDA
BURUNDI

DEMOCRATIC
REPUBLIC OF
CONGO

Aceh

Bougainville
Island

ANGOLA

MALAWI

MADAGASCAR

Moluccas

I N D O N E S I A

West Papua

PAPUA
NEW
GUINEA

ZIMBABWE

NAMIBIA

MOZAMBIQUE

EAST TIMOR

SOUTH
AFRICA

LESOTHO

AUSTRALIA

TURKEY

CYPRUS
LEBANON

SYRIA

IRAQ

ISRAEL

Cairo

KUWAIT

SAUDI
ARABIA

EGYPT

War since the Cold War
Number of wars
each year *1990–2002*

- Europe
- Sub-Saharan Africa
- North Africa & Middle East
- Central & South America
- Asia & Pacific

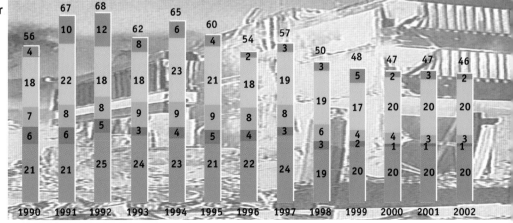

	1990	1991	1992	1993	1994	1995	1996	1997	1998	1999	2000	2001	2002
Total	56	67	68	62	65	60	54	57	50	48	47	47	46
Europe	4	10	12	8	6	4	2	3	3	5	2	3	2
Sub-Saharan Africa	18	22	18	18	23	21	18	19	19	17	20	20	20
North Africa & Middle East	7	8	8	9	9	9	8	8	6	4	4	3	3
Central & South America	6	6	5	3	4	5	4	3	3	2	1	1	1
Asia & Pacific	21	21	25	24	23	21	22	24	19	20	20	20	20

Terrorist organizations

2000–March 2003

■ active terrorist groups are based and/or have operational cells

☐ other countries

Suicide bombings

🔥 states where suicide bombers have struck

Terrorism is not different from war; it is a form of war.

In some wars in the modern age, states and non-state groups alike adopt tactics that are generally described as terrorism, such as assassinations and attacks on civilians. It has been used in Iraq as a means of defence by Saddam Hussein's regime. Predominantly, these are the tactics of the weaker side, unable to advance its cause by other means, but there is also a long history of states using terror tactics.

The tactic of suicide bombing was pioneered in recent years by Tamil secessionists in Sri Lanka. Its largest scale users are Palestinian groups fighting Israeli military occupation and control of their land. It has been used most spectacularly by the al Qaida network in its attempt to mobilize a global campaign amongst Muslims against the USA. It is not an ideology or a political creed, but a means by which some groups try to advance their cause.

Over 1,700 terrorist incidents were reported in 2002, leaving over 1,500 dead and almost 3,800 injured

Oklahoma City, USA

1995 A bomb in the Federal Building kills 168 people; the bomber reportedly believed he struck a blow for freedom.

New York and Washington DC, USA

September 2001 Al Qaida takes its war on the USA to a new level by crashing three airliners into the World Trade Center and the Pentagon. Over 3,000 people of more than 50 nationalities killed. Passengers overpowered the terrorists on a fourth airliner, and it crashed before reaching its target.

Omagh, Northern Ireland

1998 29 killed by bomb in shopping street, placed by militant Irish Republicans rejecting peace agreement. Later there is controversy about whether the security forces knew of the bomb plan soon enough to stop it.

Larba, Algeria

2002 Unknown bombers (government and armed opposition both suspected) kill 35 in a market.

Colombia

2002, 2003 Pursuing 38-year long civil war, Revolutionary Armed Forces of Colombia unleash indiscriminate mortar and bomb attacks in capital city.

USA

UNITED KINGDOM

IRELAND

SPAIN

SIERRA LEONE

LIBERIA

COLOMBIA

PERU

BOLIVIA

Terrorism

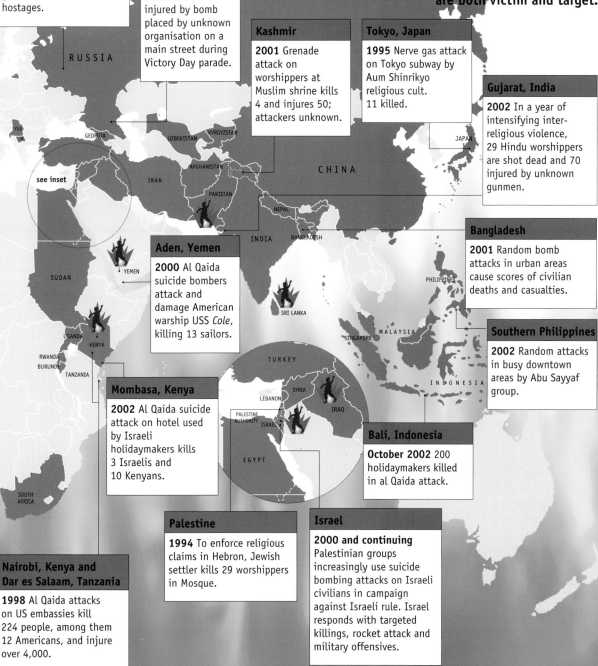

Terrorism is the use of force for political purposes, as is war. In many terrorist attacks, the victims are civilians, while the real target is the government. In some attacks, government officials and ministers are both victim and target.

Moscow, Russia

October 2002 Bringing their independence war to Russia's capital, 50 Chechen fighters hold 700 theatre-goers hostage. Rescue raid by Russian special forces kills all the guerrillas and accidentally gasses to death over 100 hostages.

Dagestan, Russia

2002 40 people killed and 15 injured by bomb placed by unknown organisation on a main street during Victory Day parade.

Kashmir

2001 Grenade attack on worshippers at Muslim shrine kills 4 and injures 50; attackers unknown.

Tokyo, Japan

1995 Nerve gas attack on Tokyo subway by Aum Shinrikyo religious cult. 11 killed.

Gujarat, India

2002 In a year of intensifying inter-religious violence, 29 Hindu worshippers are shot dead and 70 injured by unknown gunmen.

Aden, Yemen

2000 Al Qaida suicide bombers attack and damage American warship USS *Cole*, killing 13 sailors.

Bangladesh

2001 Random bomb attacks in urban areas cause scores of civilian deaths and casualties.

Southern Philippines

2002 Random attacks in busy downtown areas by Abu Sayyaf group.

Mombasa, Kenya

2002 Al Qaida suicide attack on hotel used by Israeli holidaymakers kills 3 Israelis and 10 Kenyans.

Bali, Indonesia

October 2002 200 holidaymakers killed in al Qaida attack.

Palestine

1994 To enforce religious claims in Hebron, Jewish settler kills 29 worshippers in Mosque.

Israel

2000 and continuing Palestinian groups increasingly use suicide bombing attacks on Israeli civilians in campaign against Israeli rule. Israel responds with targeted killings, rocket attack and military offensives.

Nairobi, Kenya and Dar es Salaam, Tanzania

1998 Al Qaida attacks on US embassies kill 224 people, among them 12 Americans, and injure over 4,000.

With the end of the Cold War
there was a large reallocation of
resources, from the military
sphere into the civilian economy.
Near the end of the 1990s, US
military spending started to
increase at a relatively modest
rate. Since the terrorist attacks of
September 11, 2001, a re-thinking
of the American military effort
has led to a dramatic rate of
increased spending, with
projected annual increases of
12 percent, so that the USA
dominates world military
spending to an unprecedented
degree, and spends more of its
greater wealth on the military
than the rest of the world's
richest countries.

The costs of increasing military
spending are felt in higher taxes,
reduced services from central
government, or deficit spending
that puts off the economic pain to
a later date (not much later,
though) when it will be more
severe. In broad terms, the more
that is spent on the military, the
worse will be the economic
performance over the long term.

**US military spending
increased by 30% from
1998 to 2003**

Military Spending

At over $800 billion, annual world military spending is about two thirds of what it was at the height of the Cold War in the mid-1980s.

RUSSIA

NORWAY
SWEDEN
FINLAND
ESTONIA
LATVIA
DENMARK
LITHUANIA
UNITED KINGDOM
NETH.
GERMANY
POLAND
BELARUS
BELGIUM
LUX.
CZECH REP.
SLOVAKIA
UKRAINE
FRANCE
SWITZ.
AUSTRIA
HUNGARY
MOLDOVA
SLOVENIA
CROATIA B-H
ROMANIA
ITALY
YUG.
BULGARIA
ALBANIA
GREECE
AIN

KAZAKHSTAN
MONGOLIA
NORTH KOREA
SOUTH KOREA
JAPAN

GEORGIA
ARMENIA
AZERBAIJAN
UZBEKISTAN
KYRGYZSTAN
TURKMENISTAN
TAJIKISTAN
AFGHANISTAN
CHINA

TUNISIA
MALTA
see inset
IRAN
PAKISTAN
BHUTAN
NEPAL
TAIWAN

ALGERIA
LIBYA
BAHRAIN
QATAR
UAE
SAUDI ARABIA
OMAN
INDIA
BANGLADESH
BURMA
LAOS
VIETNAM
PHILIPPINES

NIGER
CHAD
ERITREA
SUDAN
YEMEN
THAILAND
CAMBODIA

KINA SO
BENIN
TOGO
NIGERIA
DJIBOUTI
SOMALIA
ETHIOPIA
MALAYSIA
BRUNEI
SINGAPORE

CENTRAL AFRICAN REP.
CAMEROON
EQUATORIAL GUINEA
GABON
CONGO
DEMOCRATIC REPUBLIC OF CONGO
UGANDA
KENYA
RWANDA
BURUNDI
TANZANIA
SEYCHELLES
MALDIVES
SRI LANKA
INDONESIA
PAPUA NEW GUINEA

ANGOLA
ZAMBIA
MALAWI
MADAGASCAR
MAURITIUS
ZIMBABWE
NAMIBIA
BOTSWANA
MOZAMBIQUE
AUSTRALIA
SOUTH AFRICA
LESOTHO

FIJI

Inset:
TURKEY
CYPRUS
LEBANON
SYRIA
ISRAEL
JORDAN
IRAQ
KUWAIT
EGYPT

NEW ZEALAND

US military spending
Total: US$322 billion

Next ten highest military spenders
Combined total: US$314 billion

Russia 64bn, China 46bn, Japan 39bn, UK 35bn, France 33bn, Germany 27bn, Saudi Arabia 24bn, Italy 21bn, India 14bn, South Korea 11bn

Rest of the world's military spending
Combined total: US$188 billion

Budgeting for war
US military spending compared
2001

Under arms

Regular and reserve government forces
2001

☐ =1%
▫ =0.1%
▫ =0.01%

Conscription

Military service, universal or selective,
is compulsory for:

■ more than 2 years

■ 1 – 2 years

■ 6 months – 1 year

□ up to 6 months

■ voluntary military service

□ no data

**Longest compulsory service
in armed forces:** North Korea – maximum
of ten years
Lightest service: Mexico – 4 hours a week
for 12 months

The number of military personnel
does not fully show relative
military strength. Advanced
technology, better training and
superior motivation can all allow
some forces to pack a much
harder punch than numbers alone
imply. Insurgent forces are
usually much smaller than their
opponents, but often compensate
through commitment and
training.

Compulsory service often harms
military effectiveness, especially
when it means disgruntled
conscripts serving for about a
year before hurrying back to the
lives they have chosen for
themselves. There is a slow but
steady tendency towards all-
volunteer forces and, in parallel,
towards more women in the
military.

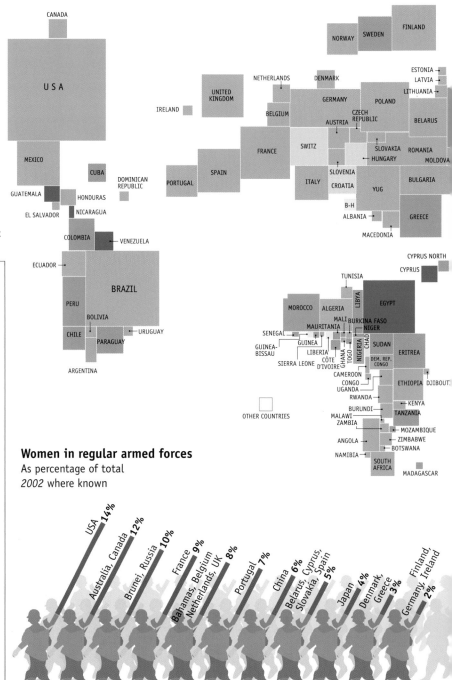

Women in regular armed forces

As percentage of total
2002 where known

USA 14%
Australia, Canada 12%
Brunei, Russia 10%
France 9%
Bahamas, Belgium, Netherlands, UK 8%
Portugal 7%
China 6%
Belarus, Cyprus, Slovakia, Spain 5%
Japan 4%
Denmark, Greece 3%
Finland, Ireland 2%

The number of regulars plus reservists serving worldwide is about the same as the population of the UK

22 million people serve in the regular armed forces – about 10 percent fewer than at the height of the Cold War in the mid-1980s.

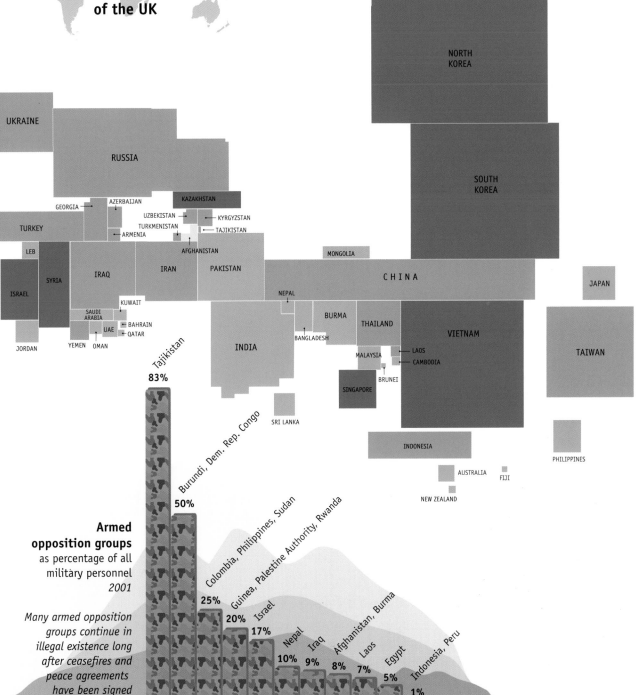

NORTH KOREA

SOUTH KOREA

UKRAINE

RUSSIA

KAZAKHSTAN

GEORGIA

AZERBAIJAN

UZBEKISTAN → ← KYRGYZSTAN

TURKMENISTAN

TAJIKISTAN

ARMENIA

AFGHANISTAN

MONGOLIA

JAPAN

TURKEY

LEB

SYRIA

IRAQ

IRAN

PAKISTAN

C H I N A

ISRAEL

KUWAIT

NEPAL

BURMA

THAILAND

VIETNAM

TAIWAN

SAUDI ARABIA

BAHRAIN

UAE

QATAR

BANGLADESH

MALAYSIA

LAOS

CAMBODIA

JORDAN

YEMEN

OMAN

INDIA

BRUNEI

SINGAPORE

SRI LANKA

INDONESIA

PHILIPPINES

AUSTRALIA

FIJI

NEW ZEALAND

Armed opposition groups
as percentage of all military personnel
2001

Many armed opposition groups continue in illegal existence long after ceasefires and peace agreements have been signed and implemented.

Tajikistan
83%

Burundi, Dem. Rep. Congo
50%

Colombia, Philippines, Sudan
25%

Guinea, Palestine Authority, Rwanda
20%

Israel
17%

Nepal
10%

Iraq
9%

Afghanistan, Burma
8%

Laos
7%

Egypt
5%

Indonesia, Peru
1%

Forces for peace

Proportion of national armed forces committed to international peacekeeping operations *2002*

- over 10%
- 1.1% – 10%
- 0.1% – 1%
- under 0.1 %
- none
- no data

Peace operations

2003

- UN peacekeeping force
- non-UN peacekeeping force

Before 1990, the UN mounted 15 peace operations. It mounted the same number in the next four years. Today, UN and other peacekeeping operations involve about 250,000 military personnel, which is a little over 1 percent of regular armed forces worldwide.

Peacekeeping operations began as a way of monitoring ceasefires and peace agreements. The troops in such operations are observers and monitors rather than fighters, and have no weapons larger than small arms, which they can only use in self-defence, when they are already being fired on and their lives are in danger.

Over the years, more complex tasks have been added, including the protection of civilians in war, which went disastrously wrong in Bosnia-Herzegovina in 1995, when peacekeepers could do nothing to prevent the massacre of 7,000 Bosniaks in Srebrenica. Helping rebuild war-torn societies is now often part of the duties of peacekeeping forces.

The first UN peacekeeping operation started in the Middle East in 1948. It is still going

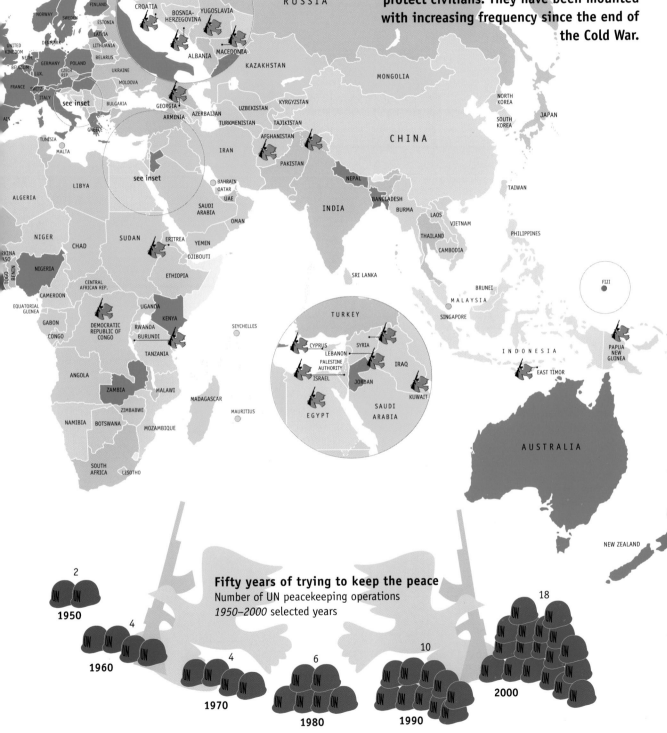

Peacekeeping

UN peacekeeping operations monitor ceasefires, implement peace agreements and protect civilians. They have been mounted with increasing frequency since the end of the Cold War.

Fifty years of trying to keep the peace
Number of UN peacekeeping operations
1950–2000 selected years

2
1950

4
1960

4
1970

6
1980

10
1990

18
2000

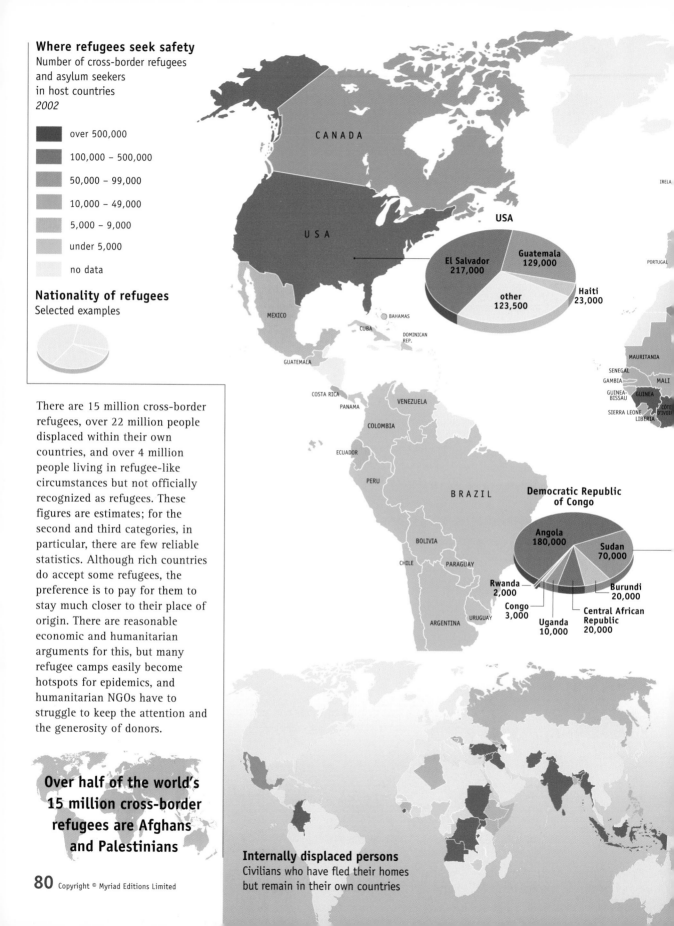

Where refugees seek safety

Number of cross-border refugees
and asylum seekers
in host countries
2002

- over 500,000
- 100,000 – 500,000
- 50,000 – 99,000
- 10,000 – 49,000
- 5,000 – 9,000
- under 5,000
- no data

Nationality of refugees
Selected examples

There are 15 million cross-border
refugees, over 22 million people
displaced within their own
countries, and over 4 million
people living in refugee-like
circumstances but not officially
recognized as refugees. These
figures are estimates; for the
second and third categories, in
particular, there are few reliable
statistics. Although rich countries
do accept some refugees, the
preference is to pay for them to
stay much closer to their place of
origin. There are reasonable
economic and humanitarian
arguments for this, but many
refugee camps easily become
hotspots for epidemics, and
humanitarian NGOs have to
struggle to keep the attention and
the generosity of donors.

Over half of the world's 15 million cross-border refugees are Afghans and Palestinians

USA
- El Salvador 217,000
- Guatemala 129,000
- other 123,500
- Haiti 23,000

Democratic Republic of Congo
- Angola 180,000
- Sudan 70,000
- Burundi 20,000
- Central African Republic 20,000
- Uganda 10,000
- Congo 3,000
- Rwanda 2,000

CANADA
USA
MEXICO
BAHAMAS
CUBA
DOMINICAN REP.
GUATEMALA
COSTA RICA
PANAMA
VENEZUELA
COLOMBIA
ECUADOR
PERU
BRAZIL
BOLIVIA
CHILE
PARAGUAY
ARGENTINA
URUGUAY

IRELA
PORTUGAL
MAURITANIA
SENEGAL
GAMBIA
GUINEA-BISSAU
GUINEA
SIERRA LEONE
LIBERIA
CÔTE D'IVOIR
MALI

Internally displaced persons
Civilians who have fled their homes
but remain in their own countries

Refugees

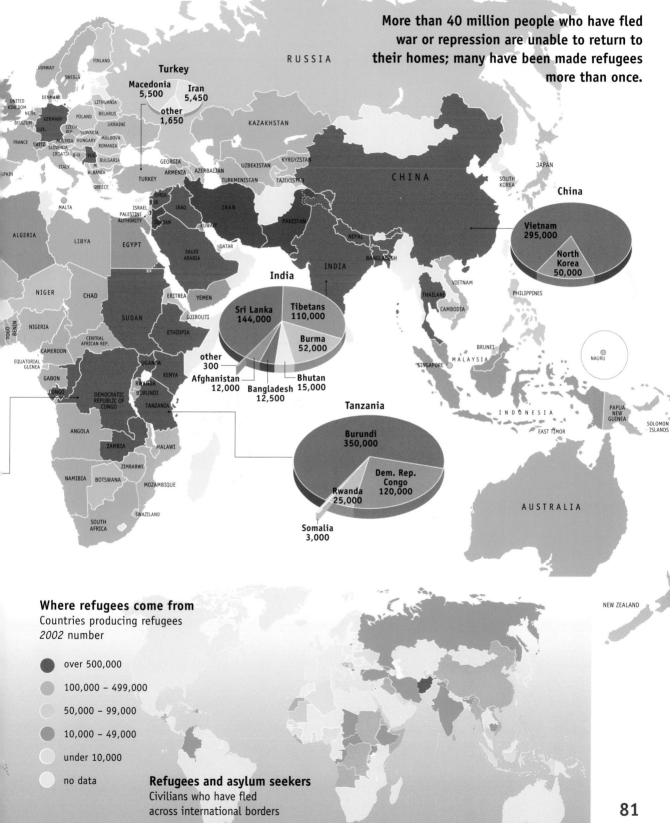

More than 40 million people who have fled war or repression are unable to return to their homes; many have been made refugees more than once.

Turkey
Macedonia 5,500
Iran 5,450
other 1,650

China
Vietnam 295,000
North Korea 50,000

India
Sri Lanka 144,000
Tibetans 110,000
Burma 52,000
Bhutan 15,000
Bangladesh 12,500
Afghanistan 12,000
other 300

Tanzania
Burundi 350,000
Dem. Rep. Congo 120,000
Rwanda 25,000
Somalia 3,000

Where refugees come from
Countries producing refugees
2002 number

- over 500,000
- 100,000 – 499,000
- 50,000 – 99,000
- 10,000 – 49,000
- under 10,000
- no data

Refugees and asylum seekers
Civilians who have fled
across international borders

81

THERE ARE VARIOUS SONGS AND SAYINGS about money – makes the world go round, source of all evil, can't buy you love, where there's muck there's brass – too many to remember them all or where most of them came from. Their profusion is not surprising, because in the world of public affairs, whether government, business or charity, there is very little that moves, for good or bad, without money.

Money, of course, is a great source of privilege and advantage – and the lack of it is quite the opposite. This is as true for governments as it is for individuals. The richest countries have the greatest room for maneuver in deploying resources to meet needs. When needs are greater than the resources to meet them, especially if available resources have been squandered, the debt trap is waiting. The problem gets worse when loans are used not for investment – to create future benefit – but for current spending, to meet the needs of today, or to pay off the problems inherited from the past. Then each additional loan gives no relief; it just drives the debtor further into the trap.

International debts and the interest on them have to be paid in a currency that can be used internationally – hard currency. For developing countries, this means exporting commodities and using the earnings for the payments. Several governments of developing countries found for a long time that one of the few exportable commodities with which they could earn hard currency was hard wood, so they cut down tropical forests, destroying their natural environment (and a potential source of future wealth) and contributing to the global problem of deforestation.

Within a purely money-based view of the world, however, there is nothing wrong with destroying forests to earn the foreign currency to make the debt payments. Everybody is acting optimally for their own interests, and as long as market prices are paid and there are no corrupt dealings, what could be wrong with that? If the forest is worth anything, somebody will pay to grow it back again.

A similar perspective can be brought to bear on the drugs trade. For a Colombian peasant or an Afghani farmer, all other things being equal, the coca bush and the opium poppy are most favorable crops. Thanks to the fact that they are illegal in the consumer countries, prices are high; despite their illegality the market is large and, from one place to another, either stable or growing. Except when growing is banned by the government – and in Afghanistan the fearsome nature of the Taliban made their ban in 2000 particularly effective – the whole business is considerably more reliable and profitable than the available alternatives. It is economically sensible behaviour, and what could be wrong with that? Of course, there are corrupt dealings, as well as a great deal of violence, but plenty of economic activities have unwanted side effects and continue nonetheless. There are, taken all round, good profits to be had in all the different links in the trading chain.

Perhaps the logic can also be extended to the trade in people? Those who make profits out of transporting people in dangerous conditions to countries where they may be able to find a job but are unlikely to find a welcome, could doubtless insist that trade is trade and profit is profit and all to the good. Most people, however, would draw the line at that, even if they let the debt system and the drugs trade slip through their moral net.

51 of the top 100 economies are corporations, not countries

The argument may seem blindingly obvious, yet it is nonetheless worth making, for many aspects of how world trade is regulated today are driven by a claim that all trade is good and the freer it is from regulation, the better. There are, indeed, good reasons in economic theory, buttressed by experience, to show that very intrusive government intervention in trade in the form either of subsidies for exports or of import barriers tends to be wasteful and counter-productive. But that is a pragmatic, empirical argument. It is different from a moral claim about trade as such. Trade is good or bad depending on what you are trading, in the same way as money is good or bad depending on how you use it.

The apostles of free trade would presumably not take their creed so far as to justify human trafficking or the illicit drugs trade. It is strange then that they often seem to find it hard to understand that other kinds of trade can also rightly be regulated and, if need be, restricted to protect nature and guard human rights, especially in poorer countries.

Purchasing power

GDP per person
2000
PPP US$

A PPP (Purchasing Power Parity) dollar has the same purchasing power in the domestic economy as $1 has in the USA.

$20,000 and over

$10,000 – $19,999

$5,000 – $9,999

$1,000 – $4,999

under $1,000

no data

Highest: Luxembourg $50,061, USA $34,142
Lowest: Sierra Leone $490, Tanzania $523

Average annual change in GDP per person
1990–2000

increase of 4% or more

decrease of 4% or more

Gross Domestic (or National) Product (GDP/GNP) is the most common way of measuring a country's wealth. It combines the value of goods (the things people make, grow or extract from the ground and then sell) and services (things people do for money). It measures the wealth in a country, but not how the wealth is distributed or used (see pages 42 and 48). Nonetheless, this crude measure of national wealth does give a broad indication of the stage of economic development reached by a country, and enables comparisons to be made between countries and across continents. It thus gives an idea of the different economic circumstances within which a government and people are working.

The average inhabitant of the world's richest country is over 100 times wealthier than the average inhabitant of the poorest

National Income

The global wealth gap keeps on growing.

Inflation
Average annual change in
consumer price index
1990–2000

- 100% and over
- 10 – 99%
- under 10%
- no data

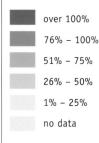

The importance of trade

Trade in goods
as percentage of GDP
2000

- over 100%
- 76% – 100%
- 51% – 75%
- 26% – 50%
- 1% – 25%
- no data

Change in trade
as share of GDP
1980–1999

increase of 100% or more

decrease of 10% or more

Some countries are so dependent on exports and imports that the value of their international trade exceeds that of their Gross Domestic Product. And with globalization, many of the wealthier counties have experienced a major increase in the scale of their international trade, which has grown much faster than their economies overall. Yet the USA, the powerhouse of the world economy and the fulcrum on which many economies balance (or come unbalanced) has a relatively low engagement in international trade. This gives the USA stability and a capacity to recover quickly from the downturn at the end of one economic cycle, ready for the start of the next cycle.

Countries with small economies, heavy trade dependence and reliance on agriculture have been hit by a change in the world market that has made fertilizers more expensive relative to agricultural products.

Bloc trade

Trade within trading blocs
as percentage of total export
of each trade bloc
2001

61% European Union

60% Free Trade Area of the Americas

73% Asia Pacific Economic Cooperation

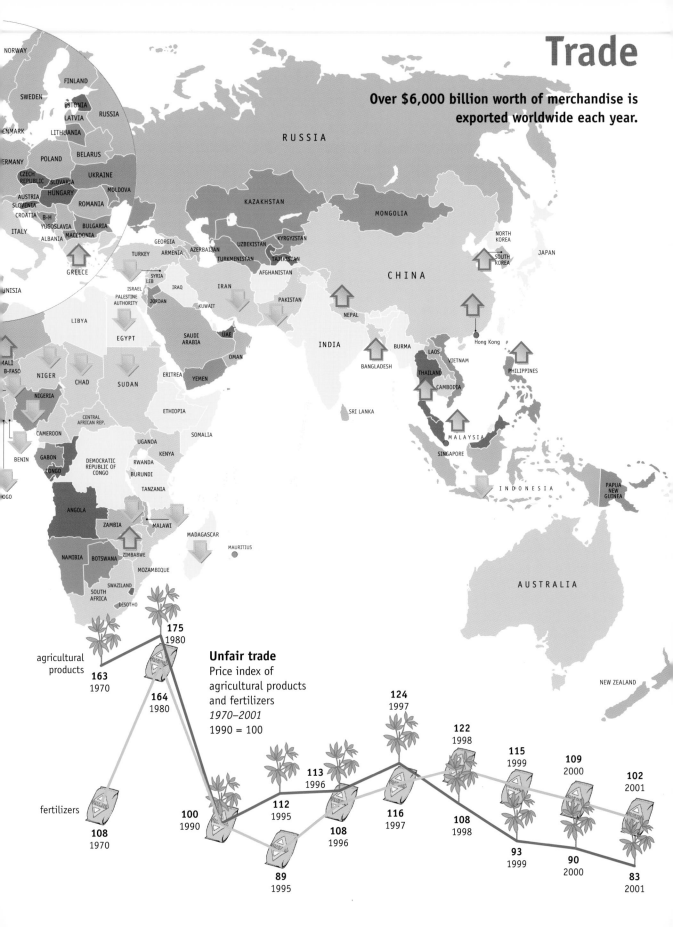

Trade

Over $6,000 billion worth of merchandise is exported worldwide each year.

NORWAY
SWEDEN
FINLAND
ENMARK
ESTONIA
LATVIA
RUSSIA
LITHUANIA
RMANY
POLAND
BELARUS
CZECH
REPUBLIC
SLOVAKIA
UKRAINE
AUSTRIA
HUNGARY
MOLDOVA
SLOVENIA
CROATIA
ROMANIA
B-H
ITALY
YUGOSLAVIA
BULGARIA
ALBANIA
MACEDONIA
GREECE
UNISIA
GEORGIA
TURKEY
ARMENIA
AZERBAIJAN
UZBEKISTAN
KYRGYZSTAN
KAZAKHSTAN
TURKMENISTAN
TAJIKISTAN
SYRIA
LEB
IRAQ
IRAN
AFGHANISTAN
ISRAEL
PALESTINE
AUTHORITY
JORDAN
KUWAIT
PAKISTAN
LIBYA
SAUDI
ARABIA
UAE
EGYPT
OMAN
NEPAL
MALI
B-FASO
NIGER
CHAD
SUDAN
ERITREA
YEMEN
NIGERIA
ETHIOPIA
CENTRAL
AFRICAN REP.
SOMALIA
CAMEROON
UGANDA
KENYA
BENIN
GABON
DEMOCRATIC
REPUBLIC OF
CONGO
RWANDA
CONGO
BURUNDI
TANZANIA
OGO
ANGOLA
MALAWI
ZAMBIA
MADAGASCAR
MAURITIUS
NAMIBIA
BOTSWANA
ZIMBABWE
MOZAMBIQUE
SWAZILAND
SOUTH
AFRICA
LESOTHO

RUSSIA
MONGOLIA
NORTH
KOREA
JAPAN
SOUTH
KOREA
CHINA
Hong Kong
INDIA
BURMA
LAOS
VIETNAM
BANGLADESH
THAILAND
PHILIPPINES
CAMBODIA
SRI LANKA
MALAYSIA
SINGAPORE
INDONESIA
PAPUA
NEW
GUINEA

AUSTRALIA
NEW ZEALAND

175
1980

**agricultural
products**

163
1970

164
1980

Unfair trade
Price index of
agricultural products
and fertilizers
1970–2001
1990 = 100

124
1997

122
1998

115
1999

109
2000

102
2001

113
1996

112
1995

116
1997

108
1998

fertilizers

108
1970

100
1990

108
1996

93
1999

90
2000

83
2001

89
1995

Debt servicing

Cost of paying interest on foreign debt
as percentage of exports
2000

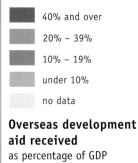

- 40% and over
- 20% – 39%
- 10% – 19%
- under 10%
- no data

Overseas development aid received

as percentage of GDP
2000

- 20% and over
- 10% – 19%

Poor countries often find
themselves saddled with debts
taken on by their former rulers,
forced to commit large parts of
their earnings from exports to
keeping up interest payments.
Irresponsible lending in the late
1970s and early 1980s is as much
a cause of the problem as
irresponsible borrowing. But the
lenders get repaid, while the
borrowers suffer – or their
subjects do, most of whom did
not benefit from loans that were
often used on the military or on
wasteful prestige projects, or
simply disappeared because of
corruption.

The phrase "debt service" is
particularly revealing of the way
the system works. What this map
shows is not the cost to poor
countries of paying back their
foreign debts, but the cost of
simply "servicing" it, by paying
the interest without paying back
any of the capital. The debt itself
remains a continuing burden. The
only way to break the cycle is to
forgive the debt.

Aid spending,
as a percentage of GNP,
is declining. The USA is the
least generous donor,
contributing
just 0.01% of its
national income.

**In 2000, developing
countries' debts amounted
to nearly $2,000 billion**

$348 — Denmark — 33%
$320 — Luxembourg — 29%
$276 — Norway — 17%
$223 — Sweden — 25%

Debt and Aid

The poorer countries of the world pay out more in interest on their debts than they receive in economic aid, most of which takes the form of low-interest loans.

RUSSIA

ESTONIA
LATVIA
LITHUANIA
BELARUS
POLAND
CZECH REP.
SLOVAKIA
HUNGARY
MOLDOVA
ROMANIA
CROATIA
BULGARIA
ALBANIA
M

KAZAKHSTAN

MONGOLIA **22**

ARMENIA **12**

17

KYRGYZSTAN

TAJIKISTAN **14**

GEORGIA
AZERBAIJAN
UZBEKISTAN
TURKEY
TURKMENISTAN
SYRIA
JORDAN
IRAN

CHINA

TUNISIA

ALGERIA

EGYPT

12

NIGER **12**

15

KINA SO

BENIN

NIGERIA

CHAD

SUDAN **29**

ERITREA

YEMEN

DJIBOUTI **13**

11

ETHIOPIA

CENTRAL AFRICAN REP. **13**

OMAN

PAKISTAN

NEPAL **11** BHUTAN

BANGLADESH

INDIA

BURMA

LAOS **16**

VIETNAM

THAILAND

CAMBODIA

13

SOUTH KOREA

PHILIPPINES

VANUATU **22**

SAMOA **12**

FIJI

CAMEROON **11**

12

GABON

CONGO

SÃO TOMÉ & PRÍNCIPE **75**

DEMOCRATIC REPUBLIC OF CONGO

UGANDA **13**

KENYA

14

BURUNDI **12**

RWANDA **18**

TANZANIA

SEYCHELLES

SRI LANKA

MALDIVES

MALAYSIA

SINGAPORE

INDONESIA

ANGOLA

ZAMBIA **27**

MALAWI **26**

COMOROS

MADAGASCAR

MAURITIUS

PAPUA NEW GUINEA

SOLOMON ISLANDS **25**

ZIMBABWE

BOTSWANA

MOZAMBIQUE **23**

SWAZILAND

SOUTH AFRICA

LESOTHO

Overseas development assistance
Amount and percentage
going to least developed countries
donated each year
US$
2000

ODA per person US$

percentage going
to least developed countries

$221	$137	$102	$91	$80	$80	$79	$71	$68	$60	$56	$55	$35	$34	$34	$30	$27	$25		
Netherlands	Switzerland	Japan	Belgium	France	Finland	UK	Germany	Ireland	Austria	Australia	Canada	USA	Spain	New Zealand	Portugal	Italy	Greece		
21%	20%	25%	15%	29%	30%	24%	31%	32%	23%	32%	23%	48%	24%	27%	12%	8%	43%		

89

Trading in narcotics

Major countries involved in
illicit narcotics trade
2000 where known

production or transport of illicit
narcotics

supply of chemicals for production
of illicit drugs

$ financial institutions
engage in currency transactions
involving proceeds from
international narcotics trafficking

Major distribution routes

← cocaine

← heroin

← ecstasy

The market for illicit drugs is very
small. Of countries for which
estimates exist, it is only in
Russia that over 1 percent of the
adult population uses opiates, and
only in the USA that over
2 percent uses cocaine. However,
the selling price is so high that
turnover and profit are huge.

The total value of the trade is
unknown because it is illegal, and
because street prices vary widely.
A UN estimate is that the total
value of the trade in illicit drugs
is well over $400 billion a year.

Criminalization of some drugs
does not restrict the trade – it just
makes criminals out of the users.
To pay for their addiction, many
heroin users become sellers
(creating new users in the
process) and turn to petty crime
and prostitution.

**The global trade in illegal
drugs is worth twice
as much as the motor
vehicle industry**

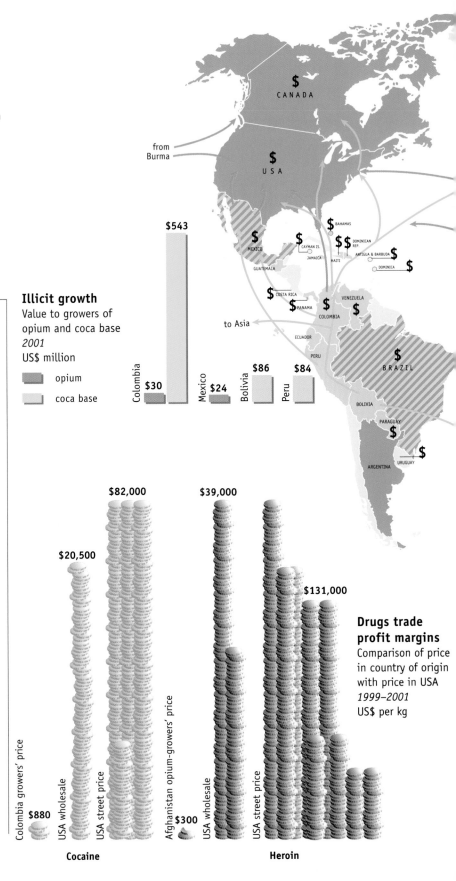

Illicit growth

Value to growers of
opium and coca base
2001
US$ million

opium

coca base

Colombia $543

Colombia $30

Mexico $24

Bolivia $86

Peru $84

Drugs trade profit margins

Comparison of price
in country of origin
with price in USA
1999–2001
US$ per kg

Cocaine

Colombia growers' price $880

USA wholesale $20,500

USA street price $82,000

Heroin

Afghanistan opium-growers' price $300

USA wholesale $39,000

USA street price $131,000

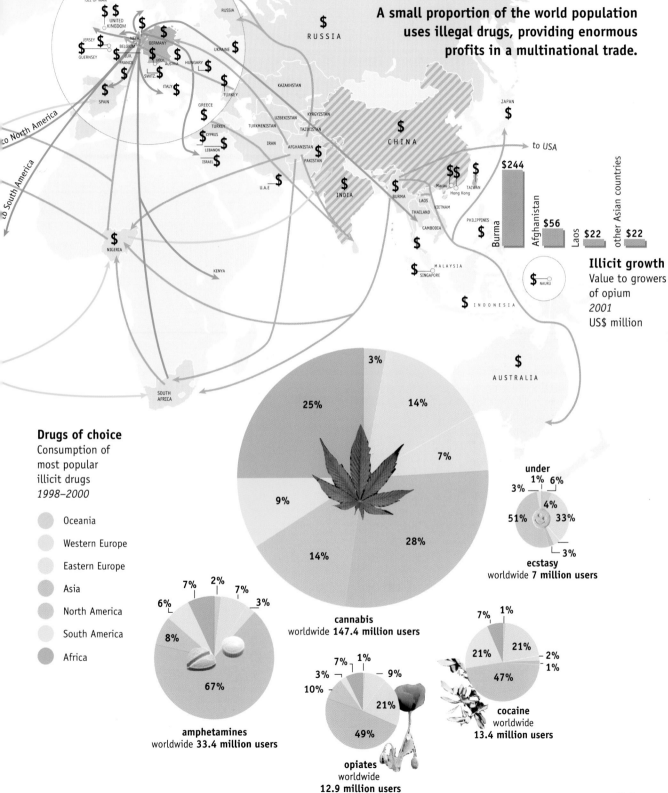

Drugs Trade

A small proportion of the world population uses illegal drugs, providing enormous profits in a multinational trade.

Illicit growth
Value to growers
of opium
2001
US$ million

Burma **$244**
Afghanistan **$56**
Laos **$22**
other Asian countries **$22**

Drugs of choice
Consumption of
most popular
illicit drugs
1998–2000

- Oceania
- Western Europe
- Eastern Europe
- Asia
- North America
- South America
- Africa

cannabis
worldwide **147.4 million users**

3%
14%
7%
28%
14%
9%
25%

ecstasy
worldwide **7 million users**

under
1% 6%
3%
4%
33%
3%
51%

amphetamines
worldwide **33.4 million users**

7% 2% 7%
6% 3%
8%
67%

opiates
worldwide
12.9 million users

7% 1%
3% 9%
10%
49% 21%

cocaine
worldwide
13.4 million users

7% 1%
21% 21%
47% 2%
1%

91

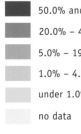
Although wealthier countries
need migrant labor – especially
the ones where the population's
average age is increasing (see
pages 26–27) – they do not
usually treat migrants well. In
many countries, there is a
bedrock of suspicion and
resentment towards people with
different appearances and
different habits and cultures,
whom it is easy to accuse of
coming to steal jobs and homes.

Migrants' journeys all too often
involve mortal dangers. On
arrival they often face low pay,
no rights (or no information
about their rights, which amounts
to the same thing), systematic
discrimination and sub-standard
living conditions. Yet there is
much evidence – not least from
the experience of the USA – that
economies flourish and cultures
benefit from the diversity of
inputs that immigration brings.

**Around 3%
of the world's population
live outside
their country of birth**

23%	15%	14%	13%	11%	7%	6%	5%	4%
Jordan	Yemen	Albania	Bosnia-Herzegovina, El Salvador, Nicaragua	Jamaica	Morocco, Sri Lanka	Sudan	Nigeria	Bangladesh

Sending money home

Workers' remittances
as percentage of GDP
of receiving country
2000

Migrant Workers

Poor economic conditions encourage migrants to leave their homes, attracted by good conditions (or the hope of them) abroad. Many take terrible risks on the journey and find a cold welcome when they arrive.

54 million
0.8 million

EUROPE

40 million
1.4 million

NORTH AMERICA

41 million
1.3 million

ASIA

13 million
0.5 million

AFRICA

6 million
0.5 million

LATIN AMERICA & CARIBBEAN

6 million
0.09 million

OCEANIA

Number of migrants
excluding refugees
2000

👤 1 million people

Comings and goings
Annual number of immigrants
less annual number of emigrants
including refugees
1995–2000
average annual rate

◀ inward flow

▶ outward flow

93

Part 7

The Business of Pleasure

IN THE RICH COUNTRIES, this is the leisure age. Working hours are shorter and holidays longer, and never have so many people had so much time with which to have a good time. The average middle-class household is filled with multiple means of using this time – television(s), video and DVD player(s), music system(s), magazines, newspapers, books and personal computer(s), let alone the paraphernalia of hobbies, sports and pastimes. All of these are commodities that are bought and sold, which means that the means of leisure and pleasure are business questions.

Pleasure is a serious business. This can be true in the sense that some ways of spending leisure time are by no means frivolous – reading to improve one's mind, for example, or much of theatre and cinema. The distinctions can get a little arbitrary at times, such as when classical music is regarded as serious and other kinds of music as trivial. The seriousness with which such interests are pursued, however, is as nothing compared with the seriousness of the average sports fan, with extensive knowledge of the history and players in the favored team, passionately argued opinions about how to improve the team's performance, savage triumphalism when the team is successful, and a rather admirable doggedness in the bad times.

Pleasure is also serious business because it is very big business. International tourism provides the holiday destination countries with foreign income – the same effect as exporting commodities. With good promotion and a flow of satisfied visitors, the tourism industry can be a major part of a country's export earnings and economic prosperity. The pleasure business functions like any other business: invest, produce, sell and reap the profits. The costs of producing major Hollywood movies are enormous and rising all the time, with profits to match if film-goers can be attracted in their millions. The fees of the biggest stars are comparably gargantuan. In sport, the same phenomenon is visible. The world game is soccer. Its best players are international stars, not just because they deliver the goods on the pitch, but because off the pitch their faces and names are recognized worldwide. Their star quality increases their clubs' profits from viewing rights, advertising and merchandizing, as long as their teams keep

16% of the world's people buy 80% of all consumables

on winning – and the fact that not everybody can be a winner is what keeps us on the edge of our seats. The star system is as real in sports as it is in cinema, although the career of sporting stars tends to be necessarily shorter than that of the major film stars.

And just like world trade in general, the pleasure business has its dark side. The trade in people that is a part of the picture of global migration has its counterpart in the sexual trafficking that is part of the picture of the pleasure business. It is, perhaps, the harshest reminder that the pleasure of consumers is not necessarily matched by pleasure for the workers in the pleasure business. The physical injuries in sports offer the same kind of reminder.

Perhaps the strangest part of the whole business of pleasure is that, although on average there is far more leisure time in the richer countries than ever before, the pace of life does not seem to have slowed. Studies indicate that people's sense of how much time they have for themselves is not so different from what it was half a century ago. People live with a persistent sense of not enough time for all the tasks they have to do, especially if combined with all the things they think they *ought* to do. On top of that the requirement to enjoy oneself just seems like one thing too many.

One of the reasons for this is that technology frees us from one task and burdens us with another. Many office workers complain about always being faced with a looming backlog of emails, because every time they respond to a message, they get a response straight back. Surveys show a high proportion of people confessing that because they spend so much time dealing with their email, they never read or consider anything properly. All response has to be instantaneous, leaving the nagging feeling that it was not the right or the best response.

And perhaps there lies the key explanation for why people report having so little time and such a pile-up of tasks and demands on them. Time is a matter of perception. Of course, the clock ticks on relentlessly, but calmness of mind can give one the feeling of having time for leisure, whereas a semi-desperate awareness of tasks not done properly leads to a feeling of not having time for anything.

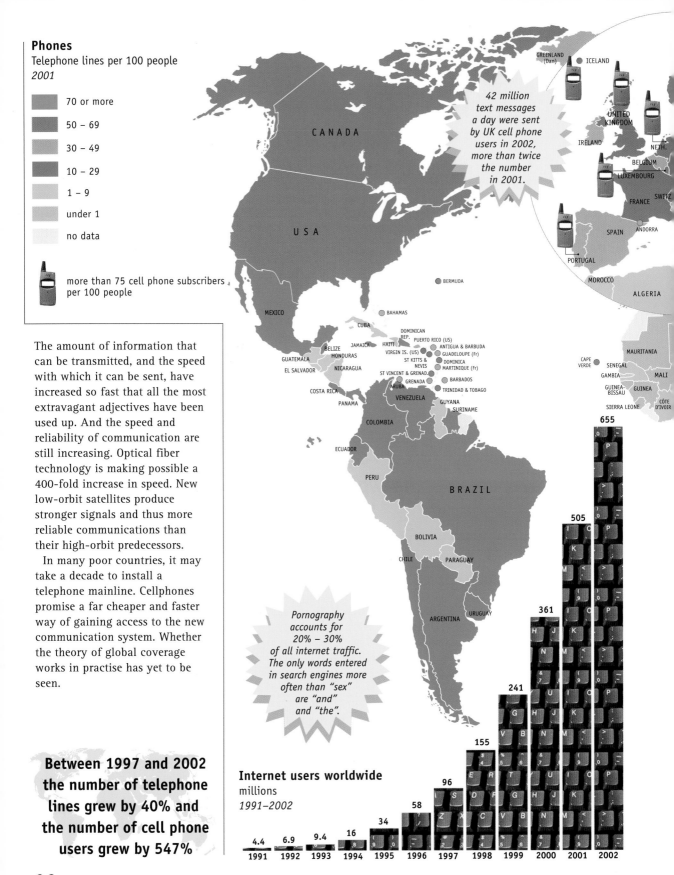

Phones

Telephone lines per 100 people
2001

- 70 or more
- 50 – 69
- 30 – 49
- 10 – 29
- 1 – 9
- under 1
- no data

more than 75 cell phone subscribers per 100 people

42 million text messages a day were sent by UK cell phone users in 2002, more than twice the number in 2001.

The amount of information that can be transmitted, and the speed with which it can be sent, have increased so fast that all the most extravagant adjectives have been used up. And the speed and reliability of communication are still increasing. Optical fiber technology is making possible a 400-fold increase in speed. New low-orbit satellites produce stronger signals and thus more reliable communications than their high-orbit predecessors.

In many poor countries, it may take a decade to install a telephone mainline. Cellphones promise a far cheaper and faster way of gaining access to the new communication system. Whether the theory of global coverage works in practise has yet to be seen.

Pornography accounts for 20% – 30% of all internet traffic. The only words entered in search engines more often than "sex" are "and" and "the".

Between 1997 and 2002 the number of telephone lines grew by 40% and the number of cell phone users grew by 547%

Internet users worldwide
millions
1991–2002

1991	1992	1993	1994	1995	1996	1997	1998	1999	2000	2001	2002
4.4	6.9	9.4	16	34	58	96	155	241	361	505	655

Communications

In 2002 approximately a quarter of a million years of time was spent on international telephone calls.

NORWAY
FINLAND
SWEDEN
ESTONIA
LATVIA
LITHUANIA
DENMARK
GERMANY
CZECH REP.
POLAND
SLOVAKIA
UKRAINE
BELARUS
AUSTRIA
HUNGARY
MOLDOVA
CROATIA
B-H
SLOVENIA
ROMANIA
YUGOSLAVIA
BULGARIA
ALBANIA
MACEDONIA
ITALY
GREECE
TURKEY
GEORGIA
ARMENIA
AZERBAIJAN
TUNISIA
MALTA
CYPRUS
SYRIA
LEB
ISRAEL
PALESTINE AUTHORITY
JORDAN

RUSSIA

KAZAKHSTAN
MONGOLIA
UZBEKISTAN
KYRGYZSTAN
TURKMENISTAN
TAJIKISTAN
CHINA
SOUTH KOREA
JAPAN

IRAN
KUWAIT
BAHRAIN
QATAR
UAE
OMAN
SAUDI ARABIA
PAKISTAN
NEPAL
BHUTAN
BANGLADESH
BURMA
LAOS
VIETNAM
INDIA
TAIWAN
Macau
Hong Kong

ALGERIA
LIBYA
EGYPT
NIGER
CHAD
SUDAN
ERITREA
YEMEN
DJIBOUTI
ETHIOPIA
NIGERIA
BENIN
CHINA SO
CENTRAL AFRICAN REP.
CAMEROON
EQUATORIAL GUINEA
SÃO TOMÉ & PRÍNCIPE
GABON
CONGO
DEMOCRATIC REPUBLIC OF CONGO
UGANDA
KENYA
RWANDA
BURUNDI
TANZANIA
ANGOLA
ZAMBIA
MALAWI
ZIMBABWE
NAMIBIA
BOTSWANA
MOZAMBIQUE
SWAZILAND
SOUTH AFRICA
LESOTHO

THAILAND
CAMBODIA
PHILIPPINES
BRUNEI
MALAYSIA
SINGAPORE
INDONESIA
PAPUA NEW GUINEA
SOLOMON ISLANDS

SRI LANKA
MALDIVES
SEYCHELLES
COMOROS
MAYOTTE
MADAGASCAR
MAURITIUS

NORTHERN MARIANA ISLANDS
GUAM
MARSHALL ISLANDS
KIRIBATI
VANUATU
NEW CALEDONIA
FIJI
TONGA
SAMOA
FRENCH POLYNESIA
MICRONESIA

AUSTRALIA
NEW ZEALAND

Europe
18

Asia
3

Americas
27

Africa
1

Oceania
40

Personal computers
per 100 people
2001 estimates

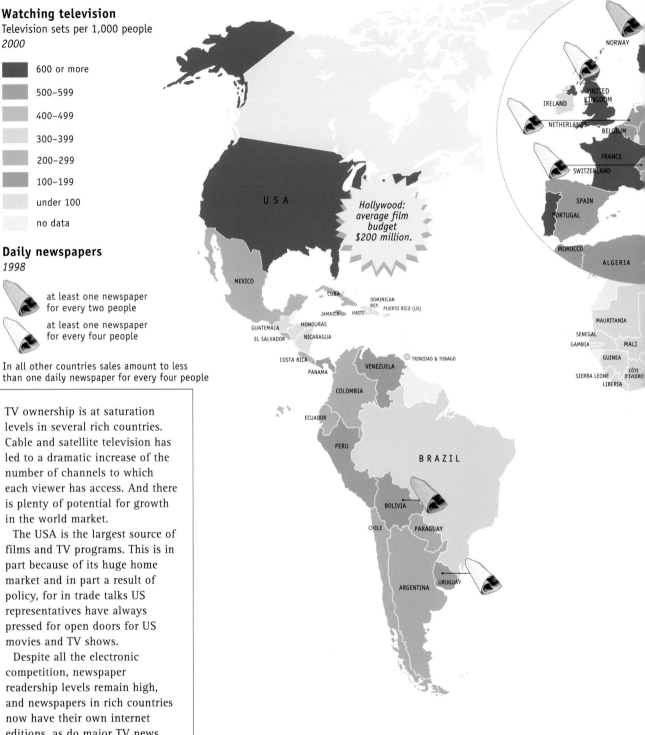

Watching television

Television sets per 1,000 people
2000

- 600 or more
- 500–599
- 400–499
- 300–399
- 200–299
- 100–199
- under 100
- no data

Daily newspapers
1998

at least one newspaper
for every two people

at least one newspaper
for every four people

In all other countries sales amount to less
than one daily newspaper for every four people

*Hollywood:
average film
budget
$200 million.*

USA

MEXICO
CUBA
JAMAICA HAITI
DOMINICAN
REP. PUERTO RICO (US)
GUATEMALA
HONDURAS
EL SALVADOR NICARAGUA
COSTA RICA
PANAMA
VENEZUELA TRINIDAD & TOBAGO
COLOMBIA
ECUADOR
PERU
BRAZIL
BOLIVIA
CHILE PARAGUAY
ARGENTINA URUGUAY

NORWAY
IRELAND UNITED KINGDOM
NETHERLANDS BELGIUM
FRANCE
SWITZERLAND
SPAIN
PORTUGAL
MOROCCO
ALGERIA
MAURITANIA
SENEGAL
GAMBIA MALI
GUINEA
SIERRA LEONE CÔTE
D'IVOIRE
LIBERIA

TV ownership is at saturation
levels in several rich countries.
Cable and satellite television has
led to a dramatic increase of the
number of channels to which
each viewer has access. And there
is plenty of potential for growth
in the world market.

The USA is the largest source of
films and TV programs. This is in
part because of its huge home
market and in part a result of
policy, for in trade talks US
representatives have always
pressed for open doors for US
movies and TV shows.

Despite all the electronic
competition, newspaper
readership levels remain high,
and newspapers in rich countries
now have their own internet
editions, as do major TV news
providers. The integration of
many media within corporations
suggests that some of the old
distinctions and divisions
between different kinds of media
will soon be breaking down.

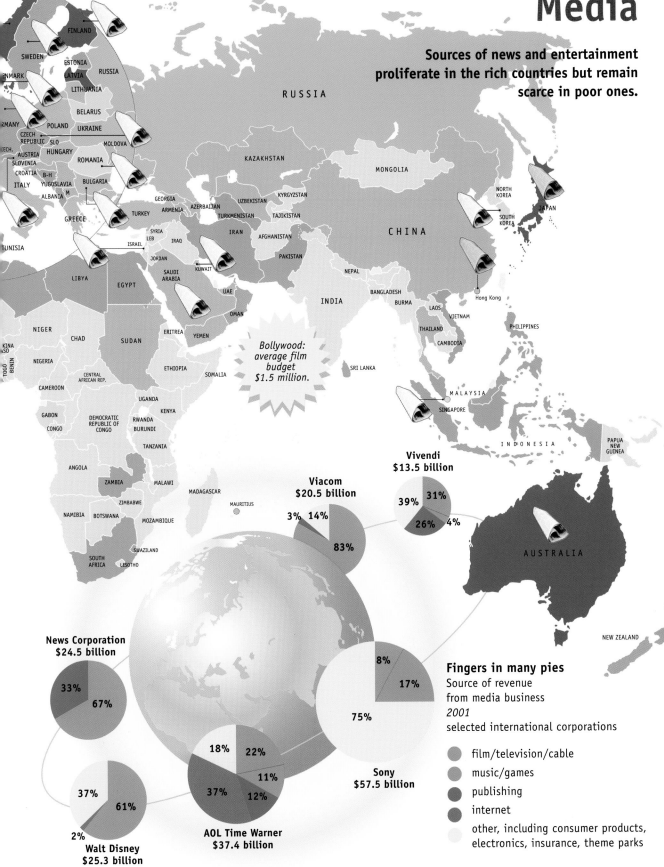

Media

Sources of news and entertainment proliferate in the rich countries but remain scarce in poor ones.

Bollywood: average film budget $1.5 million.

Vivendi $13.5 billion
31% | 39% | 26% | 4%

Viacom $20.5 billion
14% | 3% | 83%

News Corporation $24.5 billion
33% | 67%

Walt Disney $25.3 billion
37% | 61% | 2%

AOL Time Warner $37.4 billion
18% | 22% | 11% | 37% | 12%

Sony $57.5 billion
8% | 17% | 75%

Fingers in many pies
Source of revenue from media business
2001
selected international corporations

- film/television/cable
- music/games
- publishing
- internet
- other, including consumer products, electronics, insurance, theme parks

Global television broadcasting of the 2002 World Cup amounted to 41,000 viewing hours

Gate money, television fees, advertising revenue, travel (some of it international), hotels and meals, franchised goods, sporting equipment, spin-off books of top performance tips and ghost-written autobiography – sport offers multiple profit opportunities.

The reasons the stars of the major sports are paid huge sums of money – above $10 million dollars a year for those at the very top of the richest sports – is because on their shoulders rests a global industry.

Sports marketing is not just about selling a game – it is about selling places and people. A successful major sporting event like the Sydney Olympics is a major, lasting economic asset.

Football World Cup 2002
Television viewing figures
2002

 percentage of population that watched match

1.4%

USA

Mexico *v* USA
4 million

BRAZIL
Brazil *v* China
52 million

31%

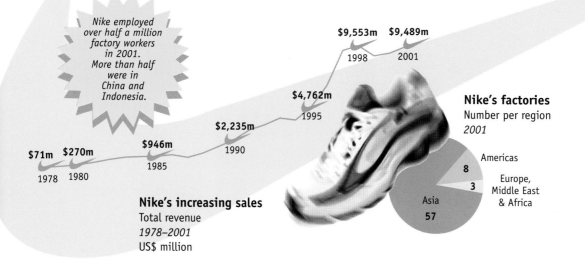

Nike employed over half a million factory workers in 2001. More than half were in China and Indonesia.

$9,553m **$9,489m**
1998   2001

$4,762m
1995

$2,235m
1990

$946m
1985

$71m **$270m**
1978 1980

Nike's increasing sales
Total revenue
1978–2001
US$ million

Nike's factories
Number per region
2001

Americas
8

Europe,
Middle East
& Africa
3

Asia
57

Sport

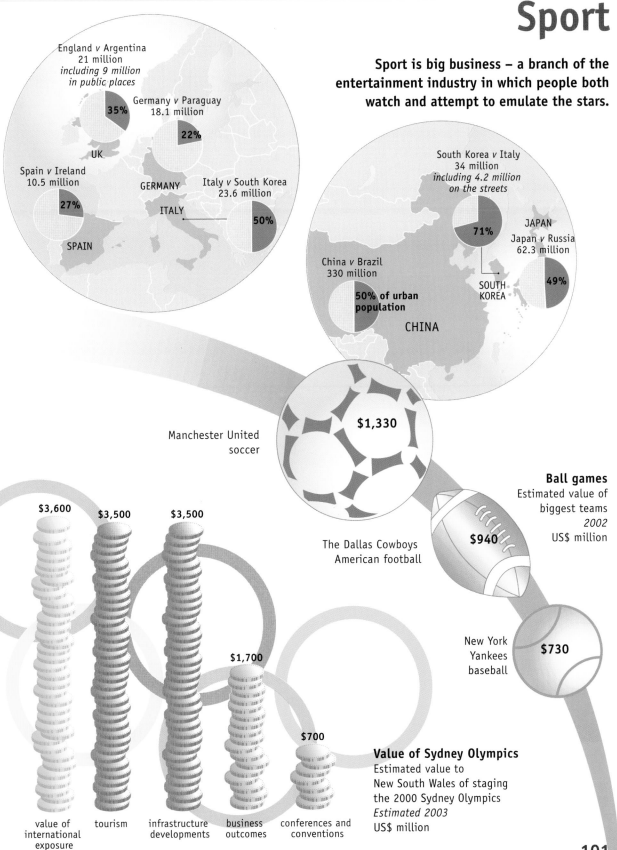

Sport is big business – a branch of the entertainment industry in which people both watch and attempt to emulate the stars.

England v Argentina
21 million
*including 9 million
in public places*

UK

35%

Germany v Paraguay
18.1 million

22%

GERMANY

Spain v Ireland
10.5 million

27%

SPAIN

ITALY

Italy v South Korea
23.6 million

50%

South Korea v Italy
34 million
*including 4.2 million
on the streets*

71%

JAPAN

Japan v Russia
62.3 million

49%

SOUTH
KOREA

China v Brazil
330 million

50% of urban
population

CHINA

Manchester United
soccer

$1,330

The Dallas Cowboys
American football

Ball games
Estimated value of
biggest teams
2002
US$ million

$940

New York
Yankees
baseball

$730

$3,600

$3,500

$3,500

$1,700

$700

value of
international
exposure

tourism

infrastructure
developments

business
outcomes

conferences and
conventions

Value of Sydney Olympics
Estimated value to
New South Wales of staging
the 2000 Sydney Olympics
Estimated 2003
US$ million

Tourism dependency

Revenue from tourism
as a percentage of foreign currency
earned from exports
2000

- 30% and over
- 20% – 29%
- 10% – 19%
- 5% – 9%
- under 5%
- no data

Most tourists come from rich countries and they are extremely demanding. Mass tourism therefore requires a well-developed infrastructure of services, based on long-term investment. The most beautiful location cannot sustain tourism on any scale if the airport is inefficient and the roads are unsafe, if the supplies of electricity and water are unreliable, the sanitation system is questionable and there is not an ample supply of delicious, fresh food. It is also helpful to have people in bars and restaurants who look as if they are enjoying serving the visitors, however grotesque the behavior of the holidaymakers. As a result, the countries that receive the most foreign tourists tend to be ones that are themselves rich.

International tourism generated US $463 billion in 2001

Tourists
Countries generating
the highest number
of tourists *2000*

Canada, Russia 18 million
France 17 million
Japan 16 million
Italy 19 million
Malaysia 26 million
Czech Republic 40 million
UK 54 million
Poland 55 million
USA 58 million
Germany 73 million

Tourism

Seeking pleasure, tourists and holiday-makers bring foreign currency to the places they visit, spend freely, and are an important economic asset to the holiday country.

Germany
19 million

Canada
20 million

Russia, Mexico
21 million

UK
25 million

China
31 million

Italy
41 million

Spain
48 million

USA
51 million

France
75 million

Destinations
Countries receiving the highest number of tourists
2000

Prostitution is said to be the oldest profession. True or not, it does seem to be an unusually resilient economic activity. It is carried out despite social disapproval, legal restrictions – pimps, prostitutes and people who pay for sex are in many countries subject to criminal punishment – and risk to the health of both prostitute and client. A similar logic applies to pornography, which continues to be traded even when it is made illegal. It is now the largest business on the internet, and results in 20 times as many videos as those released by Hollywood each year.

Beyond pornography and prostitution, sexuality is freely used to help sell a wide range of products. For products such as clothes, the connection with sexuality is evident. For others, such as cars, it is understandable. The connection between sex and chewing gum is, however, less obvious. But in a world that is equally obsessed with sex and money, the conjunction of the two is inevitable and inescapable.

The pharmaceutical business has also been successful at making money out of enhancing sexual performance, as sales of Viagra show.

Online pornography in USA
Projected growth

$400 million 2006

$230 million 2001

The global prostitution industry was worth $52 billion in 2002

Hardcore video titles
Numbers released a year in USA
1990–2001

10,800 2001
11,150 2000
10,190 1999
9,096 1998
10,190 1999
7,970 1997
7,852 1996
5,575 1995
2,475 1993
3,224 1994
1,575 1991
2,200 1992
1,275 1990

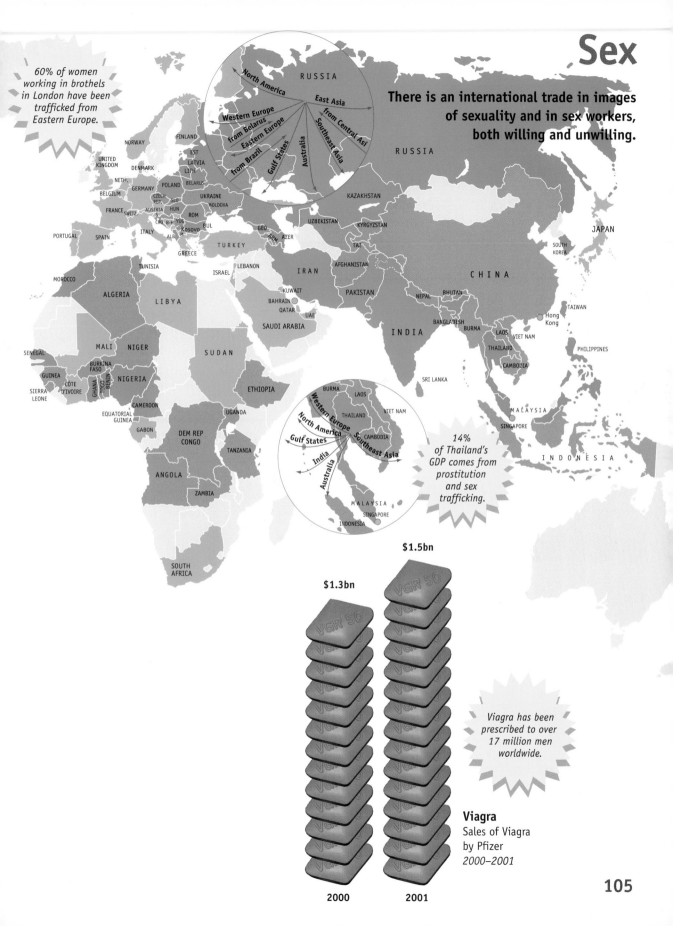

Sex

There is an international trade in images of sexuality and in sex workers, both willing and unwilling.

60% of women working in brothels in London have been trafficked from Eastern Europe.

Map inset (top) labels: North America, East Asia, from Central Asi, Western Europe, from Belarus, Eastern Europe, Southeast Asia, Australia, from Brazil, Gulf States

Map inset (middle) labels: Burma, Laos, Western Europe, Thailand, North America, Viet Nam, Gulf States, Cambodia, Southeast Asia, India, Australia, Malaysia, Singapore, Indonesia

14% of Thailand's GDP comes from prostitution and sex trafficking.

$1.5bn

$1.3bn

Viagra has been prescribed to over 17 million men worldwide.

Viagra
Sales of Viagra by Pfizer
2000–2001

2000   2001

Life and Death

MEDICAL SCIENCE AND PUBLIC HEALTH are ever advancing, and yet health remains as big an issue in rich countries as it is in poor. But while it is equally large, its shape is very different.

On the basic indicator of life expectancy, wealth means living longer. The average life expectancy is higher in richer countries, and rich people live longer on average than poor people in rich and poor countries alike. Within that picture there are variations. Some of them are based on diet; for example, the traditional diet in Okinawa in southern Japan has been shown to be very conducive to longer life, which has an effect on the Japanese statistics. Some of the variations are social. There is a solid body of research showing that not only is wealth good for life expectancy, so is social equality. The more equal a wealthy society is, the higher the average life expectancy; in a more equal society, the rich tend to live longer than their counterparts in a heavily unequal society, just as the poor tend to live longer than their counterparts at the bottom of the heap in a very unequal society. In other words, social justice is good for your health.

There are many reasons why this is so. In a more egalitarian society, there is likely to be more widespread access to health care and to health education. More importantly, however, there is likely to be a greater absorption of both care and education about health, because the self-esteem of those lower down the social scale is likely to be more resilient in general than the self-esteem of those in a comparable position in less equal societies. The gross contrasts in wealth and opportunity the latter face lead easily to a "why bother" attitude, which can be literally fatal when applied to basic issues of sanitation and healthy living.

Higher up the social scale, inequality generates intense pressures to succeed (and concomitant fear of failure) among the middle classes. Pressure can stimulate job performance, but it can also lead to an unhealthy life style – not enough sleep, food grabbed on the go, smoking to maintain some semblance of calm, and relaxing only by drinking too much. Over the years, unhealthy living leads to poor health and early death from heart trouble, high blood pressure, the heart and bronchial diseases brought on by smoking, and so on. Societies that are more egalitarian often do not perform as dynamically on the economic front, but their citizens tend to be healthier and less stressed.

Those are the ailments of societies that are wealthy overall but internally unequal. They are far removed from the ailments of societies where a large number of people are unable to find the basic necessities of daily life. In the richer countries of the world, you might assume that being able to look after yourself is a basic right, so basic it does not need to be stated in any international treaty or declaration. But in both global and historical perspective, being able to look after yourself is, if not actually a privilege, a right as often traduced as respected. Clean water, enough food, a clean place to live, sanitation, reasonably easy access to expertise (whether traditional or modern) to deal with illnesses – before we start talking about being comfortable, these are the basic necessities, and in one, several or all components, they are absent from the lives of millions of people.

One person in five is living on less than $1 a day

On top of these ailments comes the HIV/AIDS pandemic. Drugs can slow the onset of full-blown AIDS after infection but they cannot cure it, and thus far there is no inoculation or vaccination against it. The only answer is prevention, which means not having unsafe sex. But as a strategy to deal with HIV/AIDS, prevention demands education, and it demands education not only about the disease itself and how it is transmitted, but also about sexuality and its different possibilities, and about relations between men and women. Keeping healthy and keeping loved ones healthy not only means understanding sexual biology enough to use a condom, it also means understanding, confronting and getting over the difficulty between men and women of talking openly about the issue. In the wealthier countries, there are many reasons, prejudices and inhibitions that work against a proper HIV/AIDS educational strategy on a large enough scale. In poor countries, where there may be good reasons in general for skepticism in local communities about new ideas being put about by experts, there are even more obstacles and a lack of the necessary resources.

Life expectancy at birth
2000 or latest available data

- 75 years and over
- 65 – 74 years
- 55 – 64 years
- 45 – 54 years
- under 45 years
- no data

Changing life expectancy
2000 compared with 1970s

- increase of 10 years or more since early 1970s
- decrease since 1970s

Water supplies

 50% or more do not have access to improved water sources, such as a protected well, spring or tap

Nutrition, water supplies and health services are the main factors influencing life expectancy. People in richer countries therefore have a longer life expectancy than those in poorer countries, but even within the most affluent countries the rich tend to outlive the poor.

While average life expectancy has climbed as economic output has increased, two regions have seen a downturn. In Sub-Saharan Africa the decline in average life expectancy in some countries is mostly explained by the HIV/AIDS epidemic (see pages 112–113). This has a double effect: it kills people and, because it hits the economy hard, prosperity tends to decline, weakening health services.

In Eastern Europe and Central Asia life expectancy has declined as a result of the social and economic chaos that ensued in the transition from the undemocratic command economies of the old Soviet bloc.

The average life expectancy today in the poorest African countries is the same as in Japan in 1900

Life Expectancy

Growing prosperity leads to increased life expectancy. Overall, average life expectancy is rising slowly – but not everywhere.

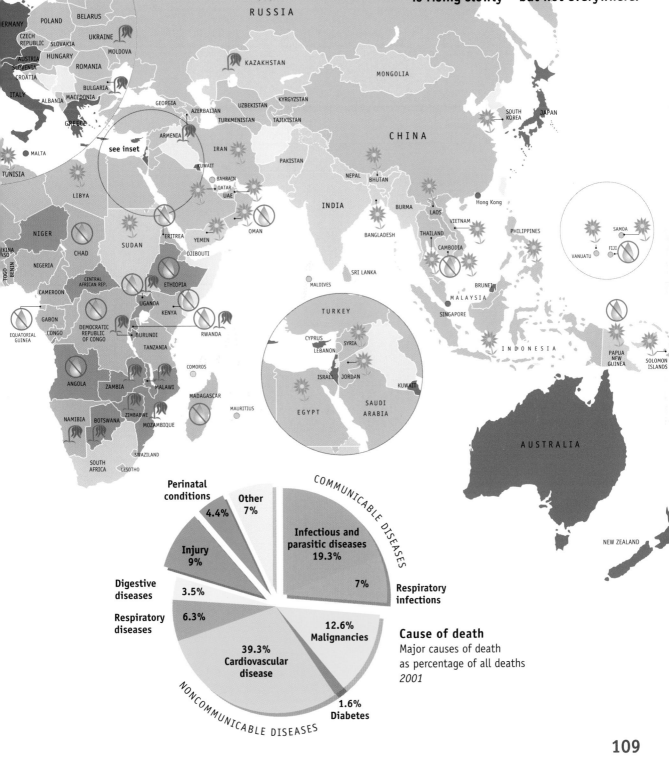

Cause of death
Major causes of death
as percentage of all deaths
2001

COMMUNICABLE DISEASES

Other 7%

Infectious and parasitic diseases 19.3%

7% Respiratory infections

12.6% Malignancies

1.6% Diabetes

Perinatal conditions 4.4%

Injury 9%

Digestive diseases 3.5%

Respiratory diseases 6.3%

39.3% Cardiovascular disease

NONCOMMUNICABLE DISEASES

Hungry children

Percentage of children under 5 years of age
moderately or severely underweight
2000

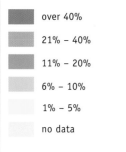

- over 40%
- 21% – 40%
- 11% – 20%
- 6% – 10%
- 1% – 5%
- no data

Undernourished adults

40% or more of population
undernourished

Each year about 9 million people die from hunger-related diseases, and the health of 2 billion people is affected by a lack of vital nutrients in their food. Yet there is in principle enough food for all. Malnutrition in the poor world contrasts with over-nutrition in the rich world. The global food market shows particularly large surpluses of grain.

One marked improvement in world affairs over the past half century is that famines now occur almost solely as the side effect of war. But the capacity to transfer large amounts of food where necessary in an emergency has not translated into an efficient and fair system in normal times.

In the richer countries, a super-abundance of calories is as much of a problem as a lack of them. Poor diet is widespread in richer countries. Obesity is a serious health issue (see pages 118–19). Eating disorders such as anorexia and bulimia are also widespread.

**Two billion people
– one third of the world's
population – suffer from
malnutrition**

Malnutrition

There is enough food in the world to feed everybody. The problem lies in the distribution. Much is wasted while many starve.

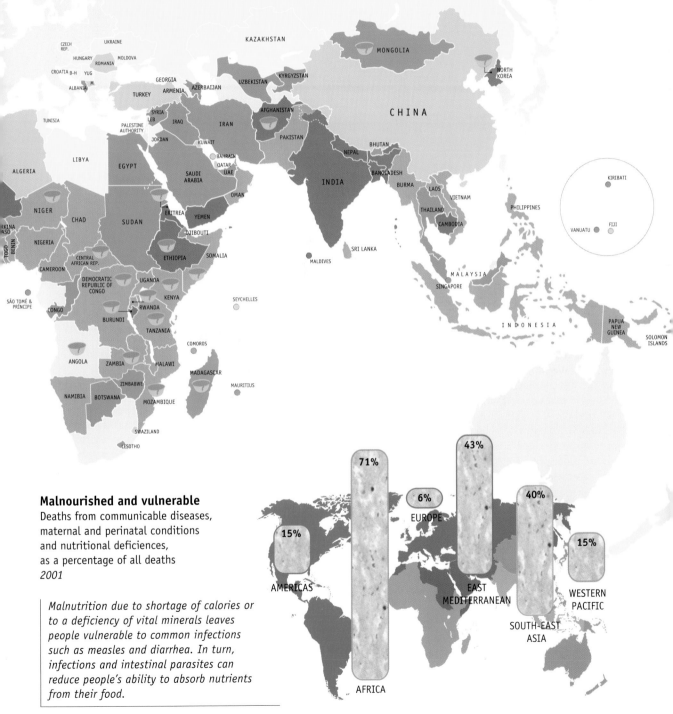

Malnourished and vulnerable

Deaths from communicable diseases, maternal and perinatal conditions and nutritional deficiences, as a percentage of all deaths
2001

Malnutrition due to shortage of calories or to a deficiency of vital minerals leaves people vulnerable to common infections such as measles and diarrhea. In turn, infections and intestinal parasites can reduce people's ability to absorb nutrients from their food.

15% AMERICAS

71% AFRICA

6% EUROPE

43% EAST MEDITERRANEAN

40% SOUTH-EAST ASIA

15% WESTERN PACIFIC

People infected with HIV/AIDS

As percentage of total population
end 2001

- 15.0% and over
- 5.0% – 14.9%
- 1.0% – 4.9%
- 0.5% – 0.9%
- under 0.5%
- no data

Highest infection rate: Botswana 39%,
Zimbabwe 34%, Swaziland 33%,
Lesotho 31%

Between 2000 and 2020,
68 million people will die of
HIV/AIDS, 55 million of them in
Sub-Saharan Africa. These
estimates, like all estimates of the
epidemic, will probably be revised
upwards as further information
becomes available.

Infection rates for young people
are two to three times faster
among women than men. The
human cost is huge; alongside the
death count, there are other
casualties of the epidemic – for
example the 1.7 million AIDS
orphans in southern Africa.

Ignorance, superstition, a
refusal by too many governments
to face the facts, and plain
embarrassment combine to make
it hard to respond to the crisis.
Inhibitions about practicing and
teaching safer sex are killing
people.

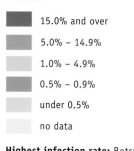

**By 2020 more people
will have died
from HIV/AIDS
than the total killed
in both world wars**

Eastern Europe and Central Asia

*Injecting drugs is
causing rates of HIV to
increase rapidly,
especially among young
people.*

Russia:
*up to 90% of infections
are attributed to
injecting drug use.*

CIS:
*almost 80%
of registered new
infections between
1997 and 2000 were in
under-29-year-olds.*

Uzbekistan:
*during the first
6 months of 2002 as
many new cases of HIV
were recorded as the
total for the preceding
decade.*

Food insecurity in the developing world

*HIV/AIDS contributes to
food insecurity because
it leads to:*
- *shortage of labor*
- *loss of wages*
- *disruption of the
  transfer of skills
  down generations*
- *additional financial
  burdens.*

The unaffordable cost of treatment

*Drugs are available that
prolong the life of a
person infected by
HIV/AIDS, but at prices
that cannot be afforded
by most people in
developing countries.*

Small signs of improvement

*Awareness campaigns,
and prevention
programs are beginning
to reduce HIV rates
among young women.*

South Africa:
*rate among pregnant
women under 20
down from
21% in 1998 to
15.4% in 2001.*

Uganda:
*rate among pregnant
women in urban areas
down from
29.5% in 1992 to
11.25% in 2000.*

Cambodia:
*rate among sex workers
down from
42% in 1998 to
29% in 2002.*

HIV/AIDS

Infection by HIV/AIDS can be prevented, but, so far, cannot be cured.

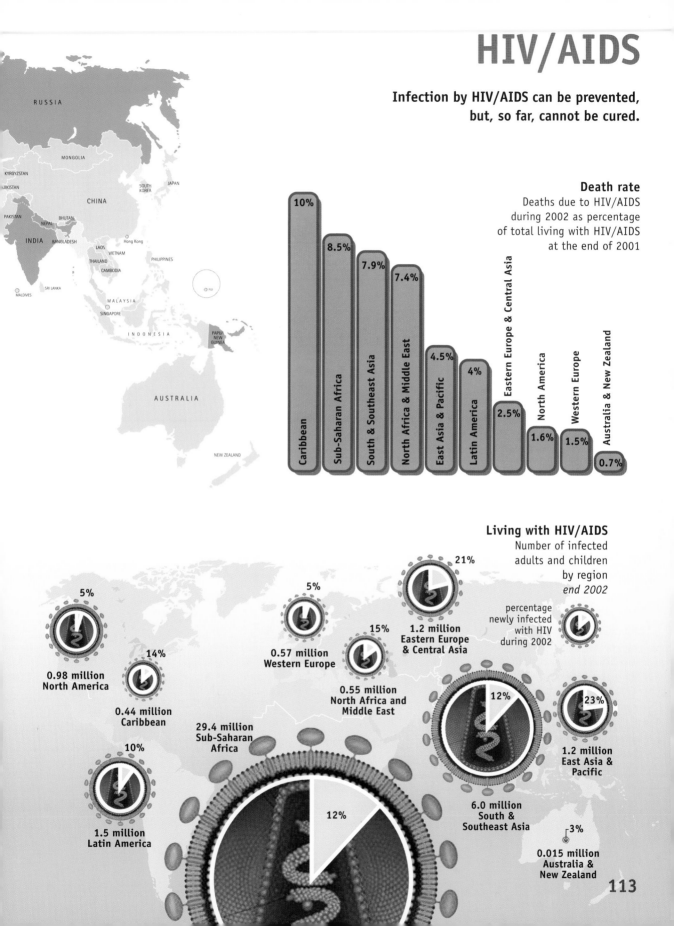

Death rate

Deaths due to HIV/AIDS during 2002 as percentage of total living with HIV/AIDS at the end of 2001

- Caribbean — 10%
- Sub-Saharan Africa — 8.5%
- South & Southeast Asia — 7.9%
- North Africa & Middle East — 7.4%
- East Asia & Pacific — 4.5%
- Latin America — 4%
- Eastern Europe & Central Asia — 2.5%
- North America — 1.6%
- Western Europe — 1.5%
- Australia & New Zealand — 0.7%

Living with HIV/AIDS

Number of infected adults and children by region
end 2002

percentage newly infected with HIV during 2002

- 5% — 0.98 million North America
- 14% — 0.44 million Caribbean
- 10% — 1.5 million Latin America
- 5% — 0.57 million Western Europe
- 21% — 1.2 million Eastern Europe & Central Asia
- 15% — 0.55 million North Africa and Middle East
- 12% — 29.4 million Sub-Saharan Africa
- 12% — 6.0 million South & Southeast Asia
- 23% — 1.2 million East Asia & Pacific
- 3% — 0.015 million Australia & New Zealand

113

Someone commits suicide every 40 seconds

In most countries 15 percent of people are likely to suffer from a mental disorder at some point during their life. Worldwide, about 200 million people have a mental illness, of whom 45 million people have severe schizophrenia or depression. Mental illness affects rich and poor people and rich and poor countries equally. The causes are currently understood as a combination of biological factors, psychological issues related to upbringing, for example, and external events that put stress on an individual.

Access to treatment is not good. There is a world average of four psychiatrists for every 100,000 people, but only one psychiatrist per 100,000 people in half the countries. In 80 countries there are no treatment facilities for severe mental disorder and no fully trained nursing staff. Forty percent of countries have no policies on mental health, 30 percent no program or government budget, and 25 percent no laws.

More than 90 percent of all suicides are associated with mental disorders. The striking difference in known suicide rates across the world is partly explained by a reluctance to record suicide as a cause of death. While suicide rates are generally highest amongst elderly men, in one third of countries young adults are now at highest risk.

Who commits suicide?
World average suicide rates per 100,000 people by gender and age range
1998

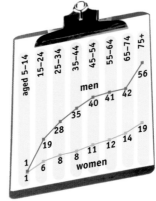

Mental health resources
Percentage of population for whom there are more than 5 psychiatric beds per 100,000 people

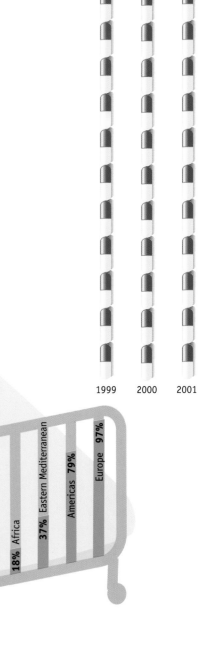

Antidepressant sales
Total world sales of antidepressants
1999–2001
US$

$11.3 billion — 1999
$13.4 billion — 2000
$15.9 billion — 2001

Mental Health

People in all countries experience mental health disorders, but attitudes and policies to the problem as well as the provision of care vary widely.

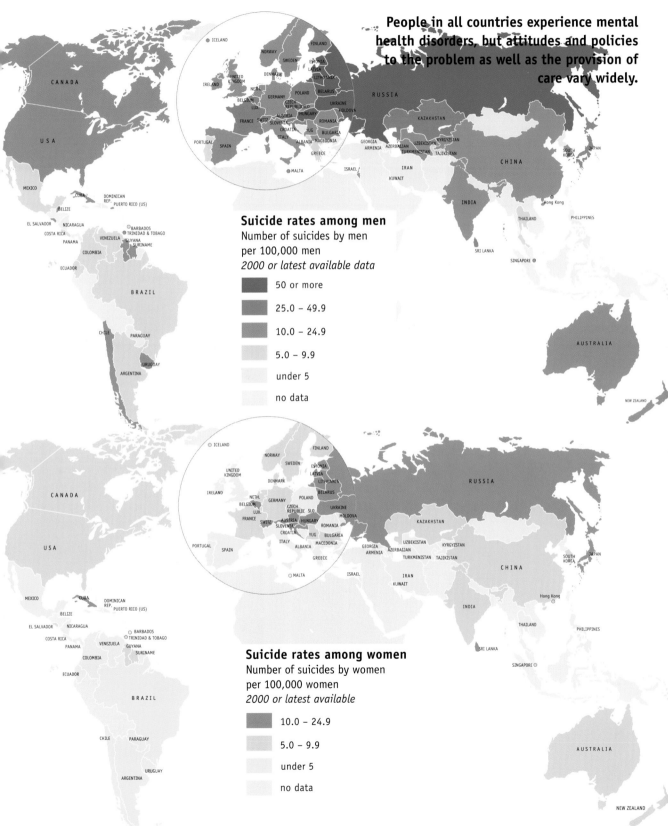

Suicide rates among men
Number of suicides by men
per 100,000 men
2000 or latest available data

- 50 or more
- 25.0 – 49.9
- 10.0 – 24.9
- 5.0 – 9.9
- under 5
- no data

Suicide rates among women
Number of suicides by women
per 100,000 women
2000 or latest available

- 10.0 – 24.9
- 5.0 – 9.9
- under 5
- no data

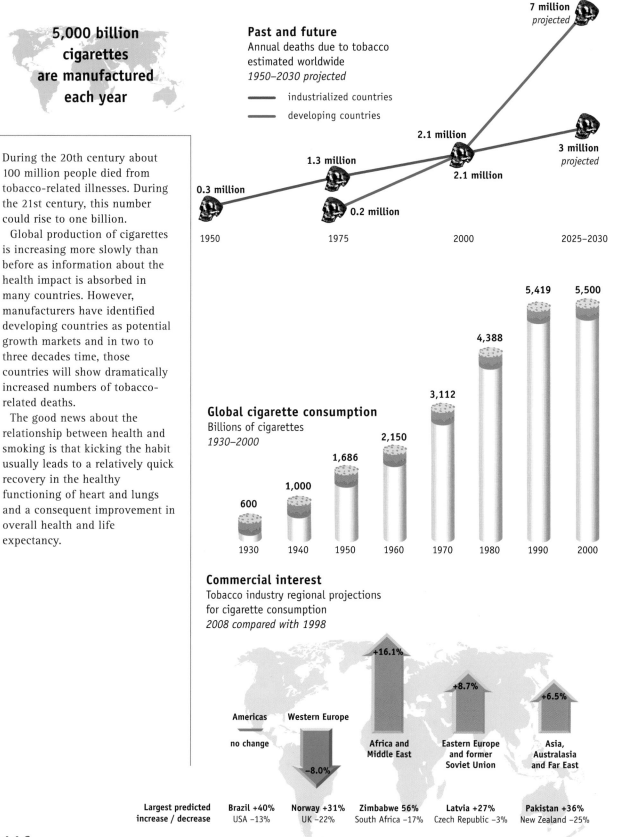

5,000 billion cigarettes are manufactured each year

During the 20th century about 100 million people died from tobacco-related illnesses. During the 21st century, this number could rise to one billion.

Global production of cigarettes is increasing more slowly than before as information about the health impact is absorbed in many countries. However, manufacturers have identified developing countries as potential growth markets and in two to three decades time, those countries will show dramatically increased numbers of tobacco-related deaths.

The good news about the relationship between health and smoking is that kicking the habit usually leads to a relatively quick recovery in the healthy functioning of heart and lungs and a consequent improvement in overall health and life expectancy.

Past and future
Annual deaths due to tobacco estimated worldwide
1950–2030 projected

— industrialized countries
— developing countries

7 million *projected*

2.1 million

1.3 million

0.3 million

0.2 million

2.1 million

3 million *projected*

1950   1975   2000   2025–2030

Global cigarette consumption
Billions of cigarettes
1930–2000

5,419   5,500
4,388
3,112
2,150
1,686
1,000
600

1930 1940 1950 1960 1970 1980 1990 2000

Commercial interest
Tobacco industry regional projections for cigarette consumption
2008 compared with 1998

+16.1%
+8.7%
+6.5%
Americas   Western Europe   Africa and Middle East   Eastern Europe and former Soviet Union   Asia, Australasia and Far East
no change   –8.0%

| Largest predicted increase / decrease | Brazil +40% USA –13% | Norway +31% UK –22% | Zimbabwe 56% South Africa –17% | Latvia +27% Czech Republic –3% | Pakistan +36% New Zealand –25% |

Smoking

Half of all life-time smokers die from tobacco-related illnesses.

Tobacco deaths amongst men
Deaths from tobacco use as percentage of total deaths among men over 35 years
2000 regional estimates

25% and over	10% – 14%
20% – 24%	5% – 9%
15% – 19%	under 5%

Tobacco deaths amongst women
Deaths from tobacco use as percentage of total deaths among women over 35 years
2000 regional estimates

15% – 19%	5% – 9%
10% – 14%	under 5%

Eating and drinking habits

colored by region
2000

Alcohol

Percentage of people over 14 years of age who consume alcohol

Fruit and vegetables

Average daily intake of fruit or vegetables by people over 29 years of age

Body mass

Average body mass index (BMI) of people over 29 years of age

Calculated by dividing a person's weight in kilograms by their height in meters squared. A healthy BMI score is between 20 and 25.

While many people in poorer countries are struggling to find enough good-quality food, in the richer countries the problem is a super-abundance of calories. Obesity is a serious health issue, leading to heart disease, high blood pressure and diabetes. It kills half a million people each year in North America and Europe. Fruit and vegetables in the diet can reduce the risk of cardiovascular disease, but low consumption may be contributing to as many as 3 million extra deaths a year in industrialized countries. Alcohol misuse is estimated to result in a further 1.8 million annual deaths.

Such problems are also increasingly being found in newly industrializing countries, where the better-off aspire to western lifestyles.

1 billion adults are overweight and 300 million are obese

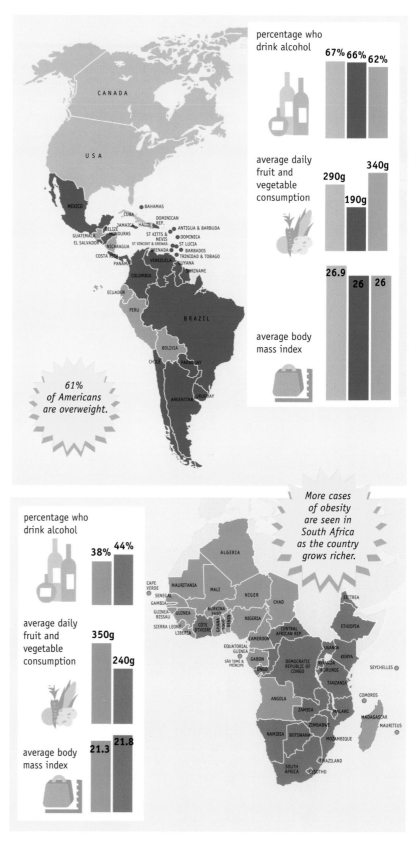

percentage who drink alcohol
67% 66% 62%

average daily fruit and vegetable consumption
290g 190g 340g

average body mass index
26.9 26 26

61% of Americans are overweight.

More cases of obesity are seen in South Africa as the country grows richer.

percentage who drink alcohol
38% 44%

average daily fruit and vegetable consumption
350g 240g

average body mass index
21.3 21.8

Rich Living

Eating too much fatty food and sugar, and drinking too much alcohol, is causing increasing health problems.

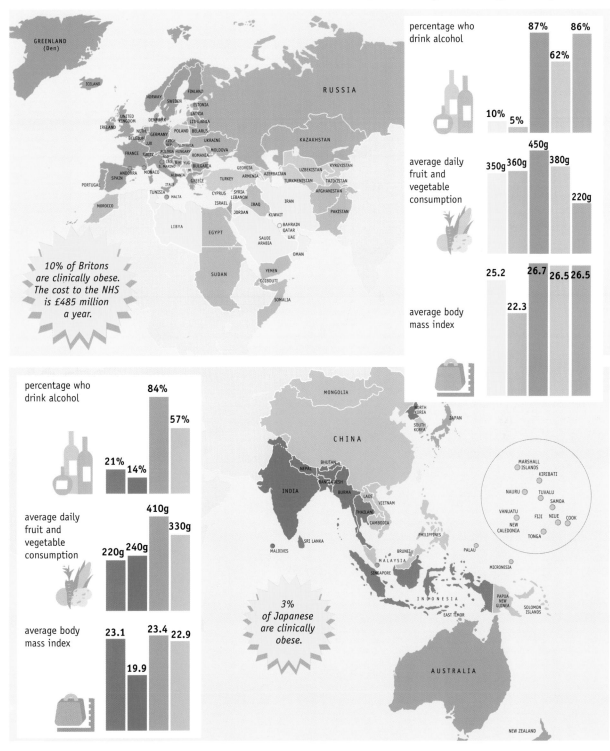

10% of Britons are clinically obese. The cost to the NHS is £485 million a year.

3% of Japanese are clinically obese.

percentage who drink alcohol
87% 86% 62% 10% 5%

average daily fruit and vegetable consumption
350g 360g 450g 380g 220g

average body mass index
25.2 22.3 26.7 26.5 26.5

percentage who drink alcohol
84% 57% 21% 14%

average daily fruit and vegetable consumption
410g 330g 220g 240g

average body mass index
23.1 19.9 23.4 22.9

THERE IS NO SHORTAGE OF INFORMATION to help us understand the world. Works of reference, annual reports, analyses of the major economic challenges and social issues of the day, statistical compilations on everything from human rights abuse and the drugs trade to how many hours people spend on-line or watching football, and the quantity of vegetables they consume – there are innumerable such sources of information, all available in bookshops, libraries and on websites. In this atlas we take an innovative approach to displaying the facts, but there is nothing different about the information itself. So it is worth knowing that there are limitations to much of the data with which we work.

Benjamin Disraeli, a political giant of Victorian England, famously exclaimed that there are three kinds of lie – "lies, damned lies and statistics!" Today he might add a few categories between damned lies and statistics – political spin and corporate accounts, for example. But his point remains valid, even though statistical techniques are vastly improved since the 19th century. Paradoxically, the statistics we use to understand the world partially obscure our view of it.

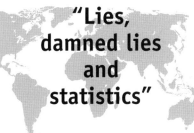

"Lies, damned lies and statistics"

To begin with, statistics are not always disinterested and objective. For example, many governments massage their employment and economic statistics to make them look as good as possible. So do some private companies. Even when there is no deceit, the raw figures may be suspect because information systems are rudimentary. Among everything we know about modern war, for example, one thing we do not know is how many civilians are killed, because in most wars no agency has the job of counting them.

Compounding these problems, some facts are pretty much unknowable. A great deal of criminal activity, for example, cannot be properly quantified precisely because it is criminal. Likewise, a great deal of legitimate economic activity also goes unquantified because it takes place outside the market economy; much of it involves the work of women, which is routinely under-reported. Sometimes, figures are produced almost at random, simply because a government minister needs a figure for an upcoming speech. If it sounds reasonable and is repeated often enough, the figure becomes a fact. Or, more precisely, it

becomes a factoid – something that looks like a fact and is treated like a fact so it might as well be a fact, sort of.

Then there is the problem of comparability. Different assumptions might lie behind statistics produced by different governments: for example, the age at which adulthood begins and what level of alcohol consumption is defined as excessive. Many of these problems have been sorted out by the international organizations that compile the data, but there are others that are irreducible. Data on ethnic and national identity are bedeviled by different and incompatible criteria. Comparisons expressed in money terms are sometimes just as complicated. A purchasing price comparison between a rich and a poor country looks at the cost in each of a fixed basket of goods. The outcome of the exercise is helpful, but the exercise itself is abstract and illusory, since in the poor country you would not even attempt to buy the same things.

The problem of problems with all this is that we do not really know which data and statistics are more reliable, which less. We might presume that, for example, economic data from western Europe are more reliable than those from less prosperous countries. Yet several European governments are suspected of manipulating their national accounts to make the budget deficit look smaller. All this should make us reflect on how statistics are used. Strong-sounding arguments are often built on weak empirical foundations, especially arguments about economic policies. Figures often contain unacknowledged areas of vagueness, so they should not be used to support very precise arguments. Trying to understand the future by extrapolating statistical trends in a straight line is usually misleading. Numbers do not prove as much as people sometimes want them to.

Many people find statistics so incomprehensible and intimidating that they will believe anything backed up by a column of numbers. But those who understand the uncertainty of statistics are skeptical when interpreting them, and circumspect when offering conclusions based on them. We do not have an alternative way to understand some important features of the complex modern world. We just have to be careful how we go about it.

Countries	1 Population		2 Children		3 Health			
	Total population 2002 millions	Urban population as % of total 2000	Infant mortality Deaths of 0 – 1 year-olds per 1,000 live births 2000	Malnutrition Underweight children under 5 years as % of total 2000	Life expectancy at birth 1995–2000 years 2000	Water % of adults not using improved water sources 2000	HIV/AIDS % of adults living with HIV end 2001	Tobacco % of adults that smoke tobacco 2000 or latest available data
Afghanistan	23.3	22%	165	48%	–	–	–	–
Albania	3.2	42%	27	14%	72.8	–	–	39.0%
Algeria	31.4	57%	50	6%	68.9	6%	0.1%	25.2%
Angola	13.9	34%	172	–	44.6	62%	5.5%	–
Argentina	37.9	88%	18	–	72.9	21%	0.7%	40.4%
Armenia	3.8	67%	25	3%	72.4	–	0.2%	32.5%
Australia	19.5	91%	6	–	78.7	–	0.1%	19.5%
Austria	8.1	67%	5	–	77.7	–	0.2%	24.5%
Azerbaijan	8.1	52%	74	17%	71.0	–	<0.1%	15.7%
Bahamas	0.3	89%	15	–	69.0	–	3.5%	11.5%
Bahrain	0.7	92%	13	9%	72.9	–	0.3%	14.6%
Bangladesh	143.4	25%	54	48%	58.1	3%	<0.1%	38.7%
Belarus	10.1	69%	17	–	68.5	–	0.3%	29.8%
Belgium	10.3	97%	6	–	77.9	–	0.2%	28.0%
Belize	0.2	48%	34	6%	73.6	24%	2.0%	–
Benin	6.6	42%	98	29%	53.5	37%	3.6%	37.0%
Bhutan	2.2	7%	77	19%	60.7	38%	<0.1%	–
Bolivia	8.7	62%	62	10%	61.4	21%	0.1%	30.4%
Bosnia-Herzegovina	4.1	43%	15	4%	–	–	<0.1%	48.0%
Botswana	1.6	49%	74	13%	44.4	–	38.8%	21.0%
Brazil	174.7	81%	32	6%	67.2	13%	0.7%	33.8%
Brunei	0.3	72%	6	–	75.5	–	–	27.0%
Bulgaria	7.8	67%	15	–	70.8	–	<0.1%	36.5%
Burkina Faso	12.2	17%	105	34%	45.3	–	6.5%	–
Burma	49.0	28%	78	36%	55.8	32%	–	32.9%
Burundi	6.7	9%	114	45%	40.6	–	8.3%	–
Cambodia	13.8	17%	95	46%	56.5	70%	2.7%	37.0%
Cameroon	15.5	49%	95	21%	50.0	38%	11.8%	35.7%
Canada	31.3	79%	6	–	78.5	–	0.3%	25.0%
Central African Rep.	3.8	41%	115	24%	44.3	40%	12.9%	–
Chad	8.6	24%	118	28%	45.2	73%	3.6%	–
Chile	15.6	86%	10	1%	74.9	6%	0.3%	22.2%
China	1,294.4	36%	32	10%	69.8	25%	0.1%	35.6%
Colombia	43.5	75%	25	7%	70.4	9%	0.4%	22.3%
Comoros	0.7	33%	61	25%	58.8	4%	–	–
Congo	3.2	65%	81	14%	50.9	49%	7.2%	–
Congo, Dem. Rep.	54.3	30%	128	34%	50.5	55%	4.9%	–
Costa Rica	4.2	59%	10	5%	76.0	2%	0.6%	17.6%
Côte d'Ivoire	16.7	44%	102	21%	47.7	23%	9.7%	22.1%
Croatia	4.7	58%	8	1%	73.3	–	<0.1%	33.0%
Cuba	11.3	75%	7	4%	75.7	5%	<0.1%	37.2%
Cyprus	0.8	70%	6	–	77.8	0%	0.3%	23.1%

Sources: **Col 1** UN Population Division; **Col 2** UN Millennium Indicator – UNICEF; **Col 3** *Human Development Report 2002*; UNAIDS; WHO: *The Tobacco Atlas, 2002*

4 Literacy	5 Media		6 Communications			Countries
% of people aged 15 and above who are literate 2000	Newspapers Number sold per 1,000 people 1998	Televisions Number per 1,000 people 2000	Telephone lines Number per 100 people 2001	Personal computers Number per 100 people 2001 or latest available data	Internet users % of population 2001	
–	5	14	–	–	–	Afghanistan
84.7%	35	123	5	0.8	0.3%	Albania
66.7%	27	110	6	0.7	0.2%	Algeria
–	11	19	1	0.1	0.4%	Angola
96.8%	37	293	22	5.3	8.0%	Argentina
98.4%	6	244	14	0.8	–	Armenia
–	293	738	52	51.7	37.2%	Australia
–	296	536	47	28.0	31.9%	Austria
–	27	259	11	–	0.3%	Azerbaijan
95.4%	–	–	40	–	5.5%	Bahamas
87.6%	–	–	25	14.2	19.9%	Bahrain
41.3%	53	7	0	0.2	0.1%	Bangladesh
99.6%	155	342	28	–	4.1%	Belarus
–	160	541	49	–	28.0%	Belgium
93.2%	–	–	14	13.5	7.4%	Belize
37.4%	2	45	1	0.2	0.4%	Benin
–	–	–	2	0.6	0.4%	Bhutan
85.5%	992	119	6	2.0	–	Bolivia
–	152	111	11	–	1.1%	Bosnia-Herzegovina
77.2%	27	25	9	3.9	–	Botswana
85.2%	43	343	22	6.3	4.6%	Brazil
91.5%	–	–	25	7.5	10.5%	Brunei
98.4%	257	449	36	4.4	7.5%	Bulgaria
23.9%	1	12	0	0.1	0.2%	Burkina Faso
84.7%	9	7	1	0.1	0.0%	Burma
48.0%	0	30	0	–	0.1%	Burundi
67.8%	2	8	0	0.2	0.1%	Cambodia
75.8%	7	34	1	0.4	0.3%	Cameroon
–	159	–	66	39.0	43.5%	Canada
46.7%	2	6	0	0.2	0.1%	Central African Rep.
42.6%	0	1	0	0.2	0.1%	Chad
95.8%	98	242	24	8.4	20.0%	Chile
84.1%	–	293	14	1.9	2.6%	China
91.7%	46	282	17	4.2	2.7%	Colombia
55.9%	–	–	1	0.6	0.3%	Comoros
80.7%	8	13	1	0.4	–	Congo
61.4%	3	2	0	–	0.0%	Congo, Dem. Rep.
95.6%	91	231	23	17.0	9.3%	Costa Rica
46.8%	16	60	2	0.6	0.4%	Côte d'Ivoire
98.3%	114	293	37	8.6	–	Croatia
96.7%	118	250	5	2.0	1.1%	Cuba
97.1%	–	–	64	25.1	22.2%	Cyprus

Col 4 UNDP, *Human Development Report 2002*; Col 5 UNESCO and International Telecommunications Union; Col 6 International Telecommunications Union

123

Countries	1 Population		2 Children		3 Health			
	Total population 2002 millions	Urban population as % of total 2000	Infant mortality Deaths of 0 – 1 year-olds per 1,000 live births 2000	Malnutrition Underweight children under 5 years as % of total 2000	Life expectancy at birth 1995–2000 years 2000	Water % of adults not using improved water sources 2000	HIV/AIDS % of adults living with HIV end 2001	Tobacco % of adults that smoke tobacco 2000 or latest available data
Czech Republic	10.3	75%	5	1%	74.3	–	<0.1%	29.0%
Denmark	5.3	85%	4	–	75.9	–	0.2%	30.5%
Djibouti	0.7	84%	102	18%	45.5	0%	–	31.1%
Dominican Republic	8.6	65%	42	5%	67.3	21%	2.5%	20.7%
Ecuador	13.1	63%	25	15%	69.5	29%	0.3%	31.5%
Egypt	70.3	43%	37	12%	66.3	5%	<0.1%	18.3%
El Salvador	6.5	60%	34	12%	69.1	26%	0.6%	25.0%
Equatorial Guinea	0.5	48%	103	–	50.0	57%	3.4%	–
Eritrea	4.0	19%	73	44%	51.5	54%	2.8%	–
Estonia	1.4	69%	17	–	70.0	–	1.0%	32.0%
Ethiopia	66.0	16%	117	47%	44.5	76%	6.4%	15.8%
Fiji	0.8	49%	18	8%	68.4	53%	0.1%	20.5%
Finland	5.2	59%	4	–	77.2	–	<0.1%	23.5%
France	59.7	75%	4	–	78.1	–	0.3%	34.5%
Gabon	1.3	81%	60	–	52.4	30%	–	–
Gambia	1.4	31%	92	17%	45.4	38%	1.6%	17.8%
Georgia	5.2	56%	24	3%	72.7	–	<0.1%	37.5%
Germany	82.0	88%	5	–	77.3	–	0.1%	35.0%
Ghana	20.2	36%	58	25%	56.3	36%	3.0%	16.0%
Greece	10.6	60%	5	–	78.0	–	0.2%	38.0%
Guatemala	12.0	40%	44	24%	64.0	8%	1.0%	27.8%
Guinea	8.4	27%	112	23%	46.5	52%	–	51.7%
Guinea-Bissau	1.3	32%	132	23%	44.1	51%	2.8%	–
Guyana	0.8	36%	55	12%	63.7	6%	2.7%	–
Haiti	8.4	36%	81	28%	52.0	54%	6.1%	9.7%
Honduras	6.7	53%	32	25%	65.6	10%	1.6%	23.5%
Hungary	9.9	65%	8	2%	70.7	–	0.1%	35.5%
Iceland	0.3	92%	4	–	78.9	–	0.2%	24.0%
India	1,041.1	28%	69	47%	62.3	12%	0.8%	16.0%
Indonesia	217.5	41%	35	26%	65.1	24%	0.1%	31.4%
Iran	72.4	64%	36	11%	68.0	5%	<0.1%	15.3%
Iraq	24.2	68%	105	16%	–	–	<0.1%	22.5%
Ireland	3.9	59%	6	–	76.1	–	0.1%	31.5%
Israel	6.3	92%	6	–	78.3	–	0.1%	28.5%
Italy	57.5	67%	6	–	78.2	–	0.4%	24.9%
Jamaica	2.6	56%	17	4%	74.8	29%	1.2%	14.6%
Japan	127.5	79%	4	–	80.5	–	<0.1%	33.1%
Jordan	5.2	79%	28	5%	69.7	4%	<0.1%	29.0%
Kazakhstan	16.0	56%	60	4%	64.1	–	0.1%	33.5%
Kenya	31.9	33%	77	23%	52.2	51%	15.0%	49.4%
Korea (North)	22.6	60%	23	60%	–	–	<0.1%	–
Korea (South)	47.4	82%	5	–	74.3	8%	<0.1%	35.0%

   Sources: Col 1 UN Population Division; **Col 2** UN Millennium Indicator – UNICEF; **Col 3** *Human Development Report 2002*; UNAIDS; WHO: *The Tobacco Atlas*, 2002

4 Literacy	5 Media		6 Communications			Countries
People aged 15 and above who are literate *2000*	Newspapers Number sold per 1,000 people *1998*	Televisions Number per 1,000 people *2000*	Telephone lines Number per 100 people *2001*	Personal computers Number per 100 people *2001 or latest available data*	Internet users % of population *2001*	
–	254	508	37	12.1	13.6%	Czech Republic
–	304	807	72	43.2	44.7%	Denmark
64.6%	–	–	2	1.1	0.5%	Djibouti
83.6%	156	97	11	–	2.2%	Dominican Republic
91.6%	43	218	10	2.3	2.5%	Ecuador
55.3%	35	189	10	1.6	0.9%	Egypt
78.7%	28	201	9	2.2	–	El Salvador
83.2%	–	–	1	0.5	0.2%	Equatorial Guinea
55.7%	–	26	1	0.2	0.3%	Eritrea
–	176	591	35	17.5	30.1%	Estonia
39.1%	0	6	0	0.1	0.0%	Ethiopia
92.9%	–	–	11	6.1	1.8%	Fiji
–	455	692	55	42.4	43.0%	Finland
–	201	628	57	33.7	26.4%	France
–	30	326	3	1.2	1.4%	Gabon
36.6%	2	3	3	1.3	1.4%	Gambia
–	–	474	16	–	0.5%	Georgia
–	305	586	63	33.7	36.4%	Germany
71.5%	14	118	1	0.3	0.2%	Ghana
97.2%	23	488	53	8.1	13.2%	Greece
68.6%	33	61	6	1.3	1.7%	Guatemala
–	–	44	0	0.4	0.2%	Guinea
38.5%	5	–	1	–	0.3%	Guinea-Bissau
98.5%	–	–	9	2.6	10.9%	Guyana
49.8%	3	5	1	–	0.4%	Haiti
74.6%	55	96	5	1.2	–	Honduras
99.3%	46	437	37	10.0	14.8%	Hungary
–	–	–	66	41.8	67.9%	Iceland
57.2%	48	78	3	0.6	0.7%	India
86.9%	23	149	4	1.1	1.9%	Indonesia
76.3%	28	163	16	7.0	0.6%	Iran
–	19	83	–	–	–	Iraq
–	150	399	48	39.1	23.3%	Ireland
94.6%	290	335	48	24.6	23.1%	Israel
98.4%	104	494	47	19.5	27.6%	Italy
86.9%	62	194	20	5.0	3.9%	Jamaica
–	578	725	60	34.9	45.5%	Japan
89.7%	77	84	13	3.3	4.1%	Jordan
–	–	241	11	–	–	Kazakhstan
82.4%	10	25	1	0.6	1.6%	Kenya
–	208	54	–	–	0.0%	Korea (North)
97.8%	393	364	48	25.1	51.1%	Korea (South)

Col 4 UNDP, *Human Development Report 2002*; **Col 5** UNESCO and International Telecommunications Union; **Col 6** International Telecommunications Union

Countries	1 Population		2 Children		3 Health			
	Total population 2002 millions	Urban population as % of total 2000	Infant mortality Deaths of 0 – 1 year-olds per 1,000 live births 2000	Malnutrition Underweight children under 5 years as % of total 2000	Life expectancy at birth 1995–2000 years 2000	Water % of adults not using improved water sources 2000	HIV/AIDS % of adults living with HIV end 2001	Tobacco % of adults that smoke tobacco 2000 or latest available data
Kuwait	2.0	96%	9	10%	75.9	–	–	15.6%
Kyrgyzstan	5.0	34%	53	11%	66.9	–	<0.1%	37.8%
Laos	5.5	19%	90	40%	52.5	10%	<0.1%	38.0%
Latvia	2.4	60%	17	–	69.6	–	0.4%	31.0%
Lebanon	3.6	90%	28	3%	72.6	0%	–	40.5%
Lesotho	2.1	28%	92	16%	51.2	9%	31.0%	19.8%
Liberia	3.3	45%	157	20%	–	28%	–	–
Libya	5.5	88%	17	5%	70.0	–	0.2%	4.0%
Lithuania	3.7	69%	17	–	71.4	–	0.1%	33.4%
Luxembourg	0.4	92%	5	–	77.0	–	0.2%	33.0%
Macedonia	2.1	59%	22	6%	72.7	–	<0.1%	36.0%
Madagascar	16.9	29%	86	13%	51.6	53%	0.3%	–
Malawi	11.8	15%	117	25%	40.7	43%	15.0%	14.5%
Malaysia	23.0	57%	8	18%	71.9	–	0.4%	26.4%
Mali	12.0	30%	142	43%	50.9	35%	1.7%	–
Malta	0.4	91%	5	–	77.6	–	0.1%	23.9%
Mauritania	2.8	58%	120	23%	50.5	63%	–	–
Mauritius	1.2	41%	17	16%	70.7	0%	0.1%	23.9%
Mexico	101.8	74%	25	8%	72.2	14%	0.3%	34.8%
Moldova	4.3	42%	27	3%	66.6	–	0.2%	32.0%
Mongolia	2.6	57%	62	13%	61.9	40%	<0.1%	46.7%
Morocco	31.0	55%	41	9%	66.6	18%	0.1%	18.1%
Mozambique	19.0	32%	126	26%	40.6	40%	13.0%	–
Namibia	1.8	31%	56	26%	45.1	23%	22.5%	50.0%
Nepal	24.2	12%	72	47%	57.3	19%	0.5%	38.5%
Netherlands	16.0	89%	5	–	77.9	–	0.2%	33.0%
New Zealand	3.8	86%	6	–	77.2	–	0.1%	25.0%
Nicaragua	5.3	56%	37	12%	67.7	21%	0.2%	–
Niger	11.6	21%	159	40%	44.2	41%	–	–
Nigeria	120.0	44%	110	27%	51.3	43%	5.8%	8.6%
Norway	4.5	75%	4	–	78.1	–	0.1%	31.5%
Oman	2.7	76%	12	24%	70.5	61%	0.1%	8.5%
Pakistan	148.7	33%	85	38%	59.0	12%	0.1%	22.5%
Panama	2.9	56%	20	7%	73.6	13%	1.5%	38.0%
Papua New Guinea	5.0	17%	79	35%	55.6	58%	0.7%	37.0%
Paraguay	5.8	56%	26	5%	69.6	21%	–	14.8%
Peru	26.5	73%	40	8%	68.0	23%	0.4%	28.6%
Philippines	78.6	59%	30	28%	68.6	13%	<0.1%	32.4%
Poland	38.5	62%	9	–	72.8	–	0.1%	34.5%
Portugal	10.0	64%	6	–	75.2	–	0.5%	18.7%
Qatar	0.6	93%	12	6%	68.9	–	–	18.8%
Romania	22.3	55%	19	6%	69.8	–	<0.1%	43.5%

 Sources: **Col 1** UN Population Division; **Col 2** UN Millennium Indicator – UNICEF; **Col 3** *Human Development Report 2002*; UNAIDS; WHO: *The Tobacco Atlas, 2002*

People and Progress

4 Literacy	5 Media		6 Communications			
People aged 15 and above who are literate 2000	Newspapers Number sold per 1,000 people 1998	Televisions Number per 1,000 people 2000	Telephone lines Number per 100 people 2001	Personal computers Number per 100 people 2001 or latest available data	Internet users % of population 2001	Countries
82.0%	374	486	24	13.2	10.2%	Kuwait
–	15	49	8	–	–	Kyrgyzstan
48.7%	4	10	1	0.3	0.2%	Laos
99.8%	247	789	31	15.3	7.2%	Latvia
86.0%	107	335	19	5.6	–	Lebanon
83.4%	8	16	1	–	0.2%	Lesotho
–	12	25	–	–	0.0%	Liberia
80.0%	15	137	11	–	0.4%	Libya
99.6%	29	422	31	7.1	6.8%	Lithuania
–	–	–	78	51.5	–	Luxembourg
–	–	282	26	–	3.4%	Macedonia
66.5%	5	24	0	0.2	0.2%	Madagascar
60.1%	3	3	0	0.1	0.2%	Malawi
87.5%	158	168	20	12.6	24.0%	Malaysia
41.5%	1	14	0	0.1	0.3%	Mali
92.0%	–	–	53	23.0	25.3%	Malta
40.2%	0	96	1	1.0	0.3%	Mauritania
84.5%	71	268	26	10.8	13.2%	Mauritius
91.4%	98	283	14	6.9	3.5%	Mexico
98.9%	154	297	15	1.6	1.4%	Moldova
98.9%	–	65	5	1.4	1.6%	Mongolia
48.9%	26	166	4	1.3	1.3%	Morocco
44.0%	3	5	0	0.4	0.1%	Mozambique
82.0%	19	38	7	3.6	2.5%	Namibia
41.8%	–	7	1	0.3	0.3%	Nepal
–	306	538	62	42.9	32.9%	Netherlands
–	207	522	47	38.6	28.1%	New Zealand
66.5%	30	69	3	1.0	–	Nicaragua
15.9%	0	37	0	0.1	0.1%	Niger
63.9%	24	68	0	0.7	–	Nigeria
–	585	669	72	50.8	59.6%	Norway
71.7%	–	563	9	3.2	4.6%	Oman
43.2%	30	131	2	0.4	0.3%	Pakistan
91.9%	62	194	15	3.8	–	Panama
63.9%	14	17	1	6.1	–	Papua New Guinea
93.3%	43	218	5	1.4	1.1%	Paraguay
89.9%	0	148	8	4.8	11.5%	Peru
95.3%	82	144	4	2.2	2.6%	Philippines
99.7%	108	400	30	8.5	9.8%	Poland
92.2%	32	630	43	11.7	34.9%	Portugal
81.2%	–	–	27	16.4	6.6%	Qatar
98.1%	300	381	18	3.6	4.5%	Romania

Col 4 UNDP, *Human Development Report 2002*; Col 5 UNESCO and International Telecommunications Union; Col 6 International Telecommunications Union

Countries	1 Population		2 Children		3 Health			
	Total population 2002 millions	Urban population as % of total 2000	Infant mortality Deaths of 0 – 1 year-olds per 1,000 live births 2000	Malnutrition Underweight children under 5 years as % of total 2000	Life expectancy at birth 1995–2000 years 2000	Water % of adults not using improved water sources 2000	HIV/AIDS % of adults living with HIV end 2001	Tobacco % of adults that smoke tobacco 2000 or latest available data
Russia	143.8	73%	18	3%	66.1	–	0.9%	36.5%
Rwanda	8.1	6%	100	29%	39.4	59%	8.9%	5.5%
Samoa	0.2	22%	21	–	68.5	1%	–	23.3%
Saudi Arabia	21.7	86%	24	14%	70.9	5%	–	11.5%
Senegal	9.9	47%	80	18%	52.3	22%	0.5%	4.6%
Seychelles	0.1	64%	13	6%	–	–	–	22.0%
Sierra Leone	4.8	37%	180	27%	37.3	72%	7.0%	18.5%
Singapore	4.2	100%	4	14%	77.1	0%	0.2%	15.0%
Slovakia	5.4	57%	8	–	72.8	–	<0.1%	42.6%
Slovenia	2.0	49%	5	–	75.0	–	<0.1%	25.2%
Solomon Islands	0.5	20%	21	21%	67.4	29%	–	–
Somalia	9.6	27%	133	26%	–	–	1.0%	–
South Africa	44.2	57%	55	–	56.7	14%	20.1%	26.5%
Spain	39.9	78%	5	–	78.1	–	0.5%	33.4%
Sri Lanka	19.3	23%	17	33%	71.6	17%	<0.1%	13.7%
Sudan	32.6	36%	66	17%	55.0	25%	2.6%	12.9%
Suriname	0.4	74%	27	–	70.1	5%	1.2%	–
Swaziland	0.9	26%	101	10%	50.8	–	33.4%	13.4%
Sweden	8.8	83%	3	–	79.3	–	0.1%	19.0%
Switzerland	7.2	67%	3	–	78.6	–	0.5%	33.5%
Syria	17.0	51%	24	13%	70.5	20%	–	30.3%
Tajikistan	6.2	28%	54	–	67.2	–	<0.1%	–
Tanzania	36.8	32%	104	29%	51.1	46%	7.8%	31.0%
Thailand	64.3	20%	25	19%	69.6	20%	1.8%	23.4%
Togo	4.8	33%	80	25%	51.3	46%	6.0%	–
Trinidad & Tobago	1.3	74%	17	7%	73.8	14%	2.5%	25.1%
Tunisia	9.7	66%	22	4%	69.5	–	–	34.8%
Turkey	68.6	66%	38	8%	69.0	17%	<0.1%	44.0%
Turkmenistan	4.9	45%	52	–	65.4	–	<0.1%	14.0%
Uganda	24.8	14%	81	26%	41.9	50%	5.0%	34.5%
Ukraine	48.7	68%	17	3%	68.1	–	1.0%	35.3%
United Arab Emirates	2.7	87%	8	14%	74.6	–	–	9.0%
United Kingdom	59.7	89%	6	–	77.2	–	0.1%	26.5%
United States of America	288.5	77%	7	1%	76.5	–	0.6%	23.6%
Uruguay	3.4	92%	15	5%	73.9	2%	0.3%	23.0%
Uzbekistan	25.6	37%	51	19%	68.3	–	<0.1%	29.0%
Venezuela	25.1	87%	20	5%	72.4	16%	0.5%	40.5%
Vietnam	80.2	24%	30	33%	67.2	44%	0.3%	27.1%
Yemen	19.9	25%	85	46%	59.4	31%	0.1%	44.5%
Yugoslavia	10.5	52%	17	2%	–	–	0.2%	47.0%
Zambia	10.9	40%	112	25%	40.5	36%	21.5%	22.5%
Zimbabwe	13.1	35%	73	13%	42.9	15%	33.7%	17.8%

Sources: **Col 1** UN Population Division; **Col 2** UN Millennium Indicator – UNICEF; **Col 3** *Human Development Report 2002*; UNAIDS; WHO: *The Tobacco Atlas, 2002*

People and Progress

4 Literacy	5 Media		6 Communications			Countries
People aged 15 and above who are literate 2000	Newspapers Number sold per 1,000 people 1998	Televisions Number per 1,000 people 2000	Telephone lines Number per 100 people 2001	Personal computers Number per 100 people 2001 or latest available data	Internet users % of population 2001	
99.6%	105	421	24	–	–	Russia
66.8%	0	0	0	–	0.3%	Rwanda
80.2%	–	–	6	0.7	1.7%	Samoa
76.3%	326	264	14	6.3	1.3%	Saudi Arabia
37.3%	5	40	2	1.9	1.0%	Senegal
	–	–	27	15.0	11.3%	Seychelles
–	4	13	0	–	0.1%	Sierra Leone
92.3%	298	304	47	50.8	36.3%	Singapore
–	174	407	29	14.8	–	Slovakia
99.6%	171	368	40	27.6	30.1%	Slovenia
–	–	–	2	4.8	0.4%	Solomon Islands
	1	14	–	–	0.0%	Somalia
85.3%	32	127	11	6.9	7.0%	South Africa
97.6%	100	591	43	16.8	18.3%	Spain
91.6%	29	111	4	0.8	0.8%	Sri Lanka
57.8%	26	273	1	0.4	0.2%	Sudan
–	–	–	18	–	3.3%	Suriname
79.6%	26	119	3	–	1.4%	Swaziland
–	432	574	74	56.1	51.6%	Sweden
–	369	548	72	–	40.4%	Switzerland
74.4%	20	67	11	1.6	0.4%	Syria
99.2%	20	326	4	–	0.1%	Tajikistan
75.1%	4	20	0	0.3	0.8%	Tanzania
95.5%	64	284	9	2.7	5.6%	Thailand
57.1%	4	32	1	2.2	1.1%	Togo
93.8%	123	340	24	6.9	9.2%	Trinidad & Tobago
71.0%	31	198	11	2.4	4.1%	Tunisia
85.1%	111	449	29	4.1	3.8%	Turkey
–	–	196	8	–	0.2%	Turkmenistan
67.1%	2	27	0	0.3	0.3%	Uganda
99.6%	101	456	21	1.8	1.2%	Ukraine
76.3%	156	292	40	15.8	33.9%	United Arab Emirates
–	329	653	59	36.6	40.0%	United Kingdom
–	213	854	66	62.3	50.0%	United States of America
97.7%	293	530	28	11.0	11.9%	Uruguay
99.2%	3	276	7	–	0.6%	Uzbekistan
92.6%	206	185	11	5.3	5.3%	Venezuela
93.4%	4	185	4	1.0	0.5%	Vietnam
46.3%	15	283	2	0.2	0.1%	Yemen
–	107	282	23	2.3	5.6%	Yugoslavia
78.1%	12	134	1	0.7	0.2%	Zambia
88.7%	18	30	2	1.2	0.7%	Zimbabwe

Col 4 UNDP, *Human Development Report 2002*; **Col 5** UNESCO and International Telecommunications Union; **Col 6** International Telecommunications Union

Countries	1 Gross Domestic Product		2 Wealth distribution	3 Trade		4 Earnings			5 Migrants excluding refugees	
	per person 2000 Purchasing Power Parity US$	annual % change 1999–2000	measured by Gini index (0 = equality) 1990s	as % of GDP 2000	% change as share of GDP 1980–99	Women's average annual earnings 2000 US$	Men's average annual earnings 2000 US$	Women's earnings as % of men's earnings 2000	Number 2000	% of population 2000
Afghanistan	–	–		–	–			–	36	0.2%
Albania	3,506	2.7%	–	35.7%	–	2,478	4,488	55%	12	0.4%
Algeria	5,308	–0.1%	35.3	53.8%	–24.6%	2,389	8,150	29%	80	0.3%
Angola	2,187	–1.8%	–	127.5%	–	–	–		34	0.3%
Argentina	12,377	3.0%	–	18.1%	154.9%	6,556	18,424	36%	1,417	3.8%
Armenia	2,559	–2.5%	44.4	61.9%	–	2,087	3,061	68%	–148	–3.9%
Australia	25,693	2.9%	35.2	34.7%	72.9%	20,977	30,449	69%	4,647	24.3%
Austria	26,765	1.7%	31.0	70.1%	72.5%	17,914	36,057	50%	741	9.2%
Azerbaijan	2,936	–7.3%	36.0	59.6%	–	–	–	–	148	1.8%
Bahamas	17,012	0.1%	–	–	–	13,344	20,779	64%	30	9.8%
Bahrain	15,084	1.7%	–	–	–	7,010	21,059	33%	254	39.7%
Bangladesh	1,602	3.0%	33.6	31.5%	130.6%	1,151	2,026	57%	966	0.7%
Belarus	7,544	–1.4%	21.7	53.0%	–	5,978	9,340	64%	1,284	12.6%
Belgium	27,178	1.8%	28.7	138.1%	44.5%	16,784	38,005	44%	860	8.4%
Belize	5,606	1.6%	–	0.0%	0.0%	2,141	8,975	24%	16	7.0%
Benin	990	1.8%	–	45.1%	–44.2%	813	1,172	69%	97	1.5%
Bhutan	1,412	3.4%	–	–	–	–	–	–	10	0.5%
Bolivia	2,424	1.6%	44.7	35.9%	46.3%	1,499	3,358	45%	61	0.7%
Bosnia–Herzegovina	–	–		87.4%	–	–	–	–	58	1.5%
Botswana	7,184	2.3%	–	92.9%	–	5,418	9,025	60%	48	3.1%
Brazil	7,625	1.5%	60.7	19.1%	72.1%	4,557	10,769	42%	543	0.3%
Brunei	16,779	–0.7%	–	–	–	10,296	22,613	46%	104	31.7%
Bulgaria	5,710	–1.5%	26.4	93.1%	–	4,587	6,898	66%	100	1.3%
Burkina Faso	976	2.4%	55.1	35.3%	–25.5%	801	1,164	69%	1,123	9.7%
Burma	–	4.8%	–	–	–	747	1,311	57%	113	0.2%
Burundi	591	–4.7%	42.5	28.6%	26.8%	490	698	70%	50	0.8%
Cambodia	1,446	2.0%	40.4	40.2%	–	1,268	1,633	78%	211	1.6%
Cameroon	1,703	–0.8%	47.7	36.5%	56.4%	1,047	2,365	44%	106	0.7%
Canada	27,840	1.9%	31.5	75.8%	113.3%	21,456	34,349	62%	5,699	18.5%
Central African Rep.	1,172	–0.5%	61.3	29.1%	–	894	1,464	61%	3	0.1%
Chad	871	–0.8%	–	33.6%	–29.4%	648	1,099	59%	23	0.3%
Chile	9,417	5.2%	56.7	51.4%	65.5%	5,133	13,786	37%	153	1.0%
China	3,976	9.2%	40.3	43.9%	–	3,132	4,773	66%	219	<0.1%
Colombia	6,248	1.1%	57.1	30.2%	80.7%	3,996	8,558	47%	115	0.3%
Comoros	1,588	–2.4%	–	–	–	1,136	2,038	56%	18	2.6%
Congo	825	–3.4%	–	105.4%	10.9%	586	1,074	55%	74	2.4%
Congo, Dem. Rep.	765	–8.2%	–	14.7%	38.2%	548	986	56%	407	0.8%
Costa Rica	8,650	3.0%	45.9	77.2%	–	4,609	12,577	37%	305	7.6%
Côte d'Ivoire	1,630	0.4%	36.7	75.9%	38.8%	868	2,355	37%	2,215	13.8%
Croatia	8,091	1.8%	29.0	64.6%	–	5,845	10,485	56%	403	8.6%
Cuba	–	3.7%	–	–	–	–	–	–	81	0.7%
Cyprus	20,824	3.1%	25.4	–	–	13,763	27,908	49%	49	6.3%

Sources: Col 1 UNDP, *Human Development Report 2002* Indicator 12; **Col 2** World Bank, *World Development Indicators 2002* 2.8 ; **Col 3** World Bank, *World Development Indicators 2002* 6.1; **Col 4** UNDP, *Human Development Report 2002* Indicator 22; **Col 5** <www.un.org/esa/population>

Economics and the Environment

6 Military spending		7 Armed forces	8 Refugees and asylum seekers	9 Energy			10 Motor vehicles	11 Water use	Countries
per person 2001 US$	as % of GDP 2001	excluding opposition forces 2001	Number in host country 2002	Amount used per person 2000 equivalent of tonne of oil	CO_2 released 2000 million tonnes	CO_2 released per person 2000 tonnes	Number per 1,000 people 2000 or latest available data	Liters per person per day 2002	
11	12.2%	50,000	–	–	–	–	–	3,287	Afghanistan
34	2.6%	27,000	–	0.5	3	1.9	44	3,287	Albania
102	6.3%	124,000	85,000	1.0	67	2.3	–	175	Algeria
109	17.0%	130,500	12,000	0.6	4.5	0.6	19	407	Angola
118	1.7%	70,100	–	1.7	130	2.1	181	–	Argentina
168	6.5%	42,060	11,000	0.5	3.6	1.7	5	2,115	Armenia
350	1.9%	50,700	21,800	5.8	329	3	530	2,116	Australia
182	0.8%	34,600	10,800	3.5	63	2.2	536	2,090	Austria
103	3.7%	72,100	7,000	1.5	28	2.4	49	800	Azerbaijan
13	0.6%	860	–	–	–	–	–	5,633	Bahamas
520	4.8%	11,000	–	9.3	14	2.2	–	–	Bahrain
5	1.4%	137,000	122,200	0.1	27	1.4	1	1,024	Bangladesh
194	2.2%	82,900	–	2.4	56	2.3	135	292	Belarus
293	1.3%	39,420	41,000	5.8	120	2	497	735	Belgium
72	2.4%	1,050	–	–	–	–	–	2,414	Belize
6	1.8%	4,750	5,000	0.4	1.4	0.6	3	1,152	Benin
9	3.8%	–	–	–	–	–	–	63	Bhutan
16	1.7%	31,500	–	0.6	7.6	1.6	41	26	Bolivia
34	3.0%	38,000	33,200	1.1	15	3.5	114	398	Bosnia–Herzegovina
127	3.8%	9,000	–	–	–	–	70	–	Botswana
61	2.1%	287,600	–	1.1	303	1.7	88	201	Brazil
833	5.5%	5,900	–	5.9	5.1	15	–	882	Brunei
46	2.8%	77,260	–	2.3	43	5.2	266	764	Bulgaria
3	1.6%	10,000	–	–	–	–	–	4,791	Burkina Faso
22	2.4%	444,000	–	0.3	8.3	0.2	–	89	Burma
5	5.5%	40,000	28,000	–	–	–	–	227	Burundi
14	5.8%	19,000	–	–	–	–	6	43	Cambodia
8	1.3%	22,100	32,000	0.4	2.8	0.2	10	109	Cameroon
250	1.1%	56,800	70,000	8.2	527	17	581	74	Canada
4	1.6%	4,150	49,000	–	–	–	0	4,017	Central African Rep.
2	0.8%	30,350	15,000	–	–	–	5	52	Chad
181	4.4%	87,500	–	1.6	48	3.2	135	63	Chile
36	4.0%	2,310,000	345,000	0.9	2997	2.4	5 ?	3,654	China
67	3.5%	158,000	–	0.7	57	1.4	51	1,123	Colombia
–				–	–	–		582	Comoros
26	3.0%	10,000	102,000	0.3	0.6	0.2	18	–	Congo
7	8.9%	81,400	305,000	0.3	2.1	0	–	36	Congo, Dem. Rep.
19	0.5%	–	10,600	0.9	4.6	1.2	133	19	Costa Rica
5	0.9%	13,900	103,000	0.4	6.3	0.4	23	3,931	Côte d'Ivoire
109	2.6%	58,300	21,900	1.8	18	4.1	–	121	Croatia
66	4.1%	46,000	–	1.2	31	2.8	32	450	Cuba
350	3.6%	10,000	–	3.2	6.3	8.4	–	1,275	Cyprus

Col 6 *The Military Balance 2002*; Col 7 *The Military Balance 2002*; Col 8 US Committee for Refugees, *World Refugee Survey 2002*; Col 9 International Energy Agency: *Key World Statistics 2002* <www.iea.org/statist/keyworld2002>; Col 10 World Bank, *World Development Indicators 2002*; Col 11 FAO Aquastats <www.fao.org>

Countries	1 Gross Domestic Product		2 Wealth distribution	3 Trade		4 Earnings			5 Migrants excluding refugees	
	per person 2000 Purchasing Power Parity US$	annual % change 1999–2000	measured by Gini index (0 = equality) 1990s	as % of GDP 2000	% change as share of GDP 1980–99	Women's average annual earnings 2000 US$	Men's average annual earnings 2000 US$	Women's earnings as % of men's earnings 2000	Number 2000	% of population 2000
Czech Republic	13,991	1.0%	25.4	120.5%	–	10,354	17,833	58%	234	2.3%
Denmark	27,627	2.1%	24.7	57.9%	55.3%	22,835	32,518	70%	233	4.4%
Djibouti	–	–3.9%	–	–	–	–	–	–	5	0.8%
Dominican Republic	6,033	4.2%	47.4	78.8%	51.5%	3,125	8,849	35%	136	1.6%
Ecuador	3,203	–0.3%	43.7	61.1%	3.1%	1,455	4,936	29%	80	0.6%
Egypt	3,635	2.5%	28.9	18.9%	–40.9%	2,003	5,227	38%	162	0.2%
El Salvador	4,497	2.6%	52.2	59.2%	48.7%	2,347	6,727	35%	24	0.4%
Equatorial Guinea	15,073	18.9%	–	–	–	8,608	21,708	40%	1	0.3%
Eritrea	837	1.1%	–	–	–	571	1,107	52%	11	0.3%
Estonia	10,066	1.0%	37.6	149.5%	–	454	885	51%	365	26.2%
Ethiopia	668	2.4%	40.0	–	–	–	–	–	462	0.7%
Fiji	4,668	0.7%	–	–	–	2,367	6,892	34%	16	2.0%
Finland	24,996	2.4%	25.6	65.5%	57.6%	20,657	29,550	70%	121	2.3%
France	24,223	1.3%	32.7	46.6%	63.1%	18,715	30,022	62%	6,144	10.4%
Gabon	6,237	0.1%	–	88.8%	2.8%	–	–	–	232	18.8%
Gambia	1,649	–0.3%	50.2	49.1%	–34.7%	1,230	2,078	59%	173	13.3%
Georgia	2,664	–12.4%	37.1	34.8%	–	–	–	–	211	4.0%
Germany	25,103	1.2%	30.0	56.3%	40.6%	16,904	33,653	50%	6,443	7.9%
Ghana	1,964	1.8%	40.7	91.4%	–1.3%	1,683	2,248	75%	601	3.1%
Greece	16,501	1.8%	32.7	32.5%	103.1%	10,185	22,998	44%	528	5.0%
Guatemala	3,821	1.4%	55.8	39.1%	–13.4%	1,836	5,772	32%	42	0.4%
Guinea	1,982	1.7%	40.3	40.2%	–	–	–	–	314	3.9%
Guinea–Bissau	755	–1.1%	56.2	83.5%	–27.9%	495	1,023	48%	12	1.0%
Guyana	3,963	5.0%	40.2	–	–	2,228	5,806	38%	2	0.2%
Haiti	1,467	–2.7%	–	29.6%	168.1%	1,049	1,902	55%	26	0.3%
Honduras	2,453	0.4%	56.3	70.9%	–21.8%	1,295	3,596	36%	44	0.7%
Hungary	12,416	1.9%	24.4	131.9%	81.8%	9,243	15,893	58%	291	2.9%
Iceland	29,581	1.8%	–	–	–	22,361	36,758	61%	15	5.5%
India	2,358	4.1%	37.8	20.3%	61.6%	1,267	3,383	37%	6,100	0.6%
Indonesia	3,043	2.5%	31.7	62.4%	–16.5%	2,053	4,026	51%	275	0.1%
Iran	5,884	1.9%	–	43.1%	–63.3%	2,524	9,088	28%	453	0.6%
Iraq	–	–	–	–	–	–	–	–	19	0.1%
Ireland	29,866	6.5%	35.9	139.3%	129.1%	17,078	42,815	40%	307	8.1%
Israel	20,131	2.2%	38.1	62.9%	25.1%	13,864	26,565	52%	2,252	37.3%
Italy	23,626	1.4%	27.3	44.2%	68.5%	14,719	33,084	44%	1,627	2.8%
Jamaica	3,639	–0.4%	37.9	60.9%	42.2%	2,900	4,400	66%	13	0.5%
Japan	26,755	1.1%	24.9	17.7%	39.3%	16,601	37,345	44%	1,616	1.3%
Jordan	3,966	1.0%	36.4	77.2%	–7.3%	1,749	6,014	29%	334	6.8%
Kazakhstan	5,871	–3.1%	35.4	77.8%	–	–	–	–	3,007	18.6%
Kenya	1,022	–0.5%	44.9	46.7%	–9.1%	975	1,069	91%	121	0.4%
Korea (North)	–	–	–	–	–	–	–	–	37	0.2%
Korea (South)	17,380	4.7%	31.6	72.8%	121.6%	10,791	23,884	45%	597	1.3%

Sources: **Col 1** UNDP, *Human Development Report 2002* Indicator 12; **Col 2** World Bank, *World Development Indicators 2002* 2.8 ; **Col 3** World Bank, *World Development Indicators 2002* 6.1; **Col 4** UNDP, *Human Development Report 2002* Indicator 22; **Col 5** <www.un.org/esa/population>

Economics and the Environment

6 Military spending		7 Armed forces	8 Refugees and asylum seekers	9 Energy			10 Motor vehicles	11 Water use	Countries
per person 2001 US$	as % of GDP 2001	excluding opposition forces 2001	Number in host country 2002	Amount used per person 2000 equivalent of tonne of oil	CO_2 released 2000 million tonnes	CO_2 released per person 2000 tonnes	Number per 1,000 people 2000 or latest available data	Liters per person per day 2002	
113	2.2%	53,600	10,600	3.9	119	12	363	738	Czech Republic
454	1.5%	21,400	12,200	3.6	50	9.4	411	731	Denmark
35	3.9%	9,600	22,000	–	–	–	–	618	Djibouti
18	0.7%	24,500	–	0.9	18	2.1	75	33	Dominican Republic
39	2.9%	59,500	–	0.7	17	1.4	46	2,729	Ecuador
62	4.7%	443,000	75,000	0.7	108	1.7	29	3,680	Egypt
26	1.2%	16,800	–	0.7	5.2	0.8	61	2,224	El Salvador
9	0.3%	1,320	–	–	–	–	–	318	Equatorial Guinea
45	20.9%	171,900	–	0.2	0.6	0.1	–	60	Eritrea
66	1.7%	4,450	–	3.3	14	10	394	–	Estonia
9	9.8%	252,500	114,000	0.3	3.2	0.1	2	311	Ethiopia
33	1.6%	3,500	–	–	–	–	–	96	Fiji
275	1.2%	32,250	–	6.4	55	11	462	101	Finland
553	2.6%	273,740	12,400	4.3	373	6.2	564	1,165	France
93	2.4%	4,700	20,000	1.3	1.4	1.1	–	1,745	Gabon
2	0.7%	800	15,000	–	–	–	14	134	Gambia
51	1.7%	16,790	7,900	0.6	6	1.2	63	42	Georgia
328	1.5%	308,400	116,000	4.1	833	10	405	1,806	Germany
2	0.7%	7,000	12,000	0.4	4.7	0.2	–	1,546	Ghana
520	4.8%	159,170	6,500	2.6	88	8.3	348	43	Greece
16	0.9%	31,400	–	0.6	8.8	0.8	57	1,301	Guatemala
5	1.5%	9,700	190,000	–	–	–	4	279	Guinea
2	1.5%	9,250	7,000	–	–	–	7	249	Guinea–Bissau
7	0.9%	1,600	–	–	–	–	–	38	Guyana
5	1.1%	–	–	0.3	1.4	0.2	–	5,260	Haiti
15	1.5%	8,300	–	0.5	4.4	0.7	62	330	Honduras
92	1.8%	33,810	–	2.5	55	5.5	272	649	Hungary
–	–	–	–	12.2	2.2	7.7	–	1,872	Iceland
14	2.9%	1,263,000	345,800	0.5	937	0.9	8	1,570	India
4	0.6%	297,000	81,300	0.7	269	1.3	25	1,358	Indonesia
66	5.8%	513,000	2,558,000	1.8	292	4.6	–	960	Iran
58	9.3%	424,000	–	1.2	77	3.3	–	2,728	Iraq
164	0.5%	10,460	9,500	3.9	41	11	270	5,110	Ireland
1,673	9.5%	163,500	–	3.2	62	10	270	569	Israel
365	2.0%	230,350	9,600	3.0	426	7.4	591	862	Italy
16	0.5%	2,830	–	1.5	9.8	3.7	–	2,676	Jamaica
310	1.0%	239,800	6,400	4.1	1155	9.1	560	957	Japan
145	8.5%	100,240	1,643,900	1.1	14	2.9	60	1,970	Jordan
79	1.3%	64,000	19,500	2.6	123	8.3	86	549	Kazakhstan
10	3.1%	24,400	243,000	0.5	9.3	0.3	13	5,705	Kenya
91	11.6%	683,000	–	2.1	167	7.5	–	183	Korea (North)
237	2.7%	1,082,000	–	4.1	434	9.2	238	1,742	Korea (South)

Col 6 *The Military Balance 2002*; **Col 7** *The Military Balance 2002*; **Col 8** US Committee for Refugees, *World Refugee Survey 2002*; **Col 9** International Energy Agency: *Key World Statistics 2002* <www.iea.org/statist/keyworld2002>; **Col 10** World Bank, *World Development Indicators 2002*; **Col 11** FAO Aquastats <www.fao.org>

Countries	1 Gross Domestic Product		2 Wealth distribution	3 Trade		4 Earnings			5 Migrants excluding refugees	
	per person 2000 Purchasing Power Parity US$	annual % change 1999–2000	measured by Gini index (0 = equality) 1990s	as % of GDP 2000	% change as share of GDP 1980–99	Women's average annual earnings 2000 US$	Men's average annual earnings 2000 US$	Women's earnings as % of men's earnings 2000	Number 2000	% of population 2000
Kuwait	15,799	−1.4%	–	71.9%	–	6,895	22,186	31%	1,105	57.7%
Kyrgyzstan	2,711	−5.1%	34.6	81.3%	–	–	–	–	561	11.4%
Laos	1,575	3.9%	37.0	52.7%	–	1,242	1,909	65%	16	0.3%
Latvia	7,045	−2.3%	32.4	70.7%	–	5,992	8,276	72%	613	25.3%
Lebanon	4,308	4.2%	–	42.1%	–	2,013	6,704	30%	251	7.2%
Lesotho	2,031	2.1%	56.0	100.1%	0.9%	1,223	2,853	43%	6	0.3%
Liberia	–	–	–	–	–	–	–	–	90	3.1%
Libya	–	–	–	–	–	2,921	11,894	25%	558	10.6%
Lithuania	7,106	−2.9%	32.4	81.9%	–	5,789	8,582	67%	339	9.2%
Luxembourg	50,061	4.1%	26.9	–	–	27,396	73,465	37%	162	37.0%
Macedonia	5,086	−1.5%	–	100.3%	–	–	–	–	24	1.2%
Madagascar	840	−0.9%	38.1	24.8%	−25.1%	624	1,059	59%	61	0.4%
Malawi	615	1.8%	–	55.4%	−32.4%	506	726	70%	276	2.4%
Malaysia	9,068	4.4%	49.2	201.3%	124.8%	5,711	12,338	46%	1,342	6.0%
Mali	797	1.3%	50.5	54.0%	125.5%	606	992	61%	40	0.3%
Malta	17,273	4.0%	–	–	–	7,626	27,104	28%	9	2.2%
Mauritania	1,677	1.2%	37.3	68.5%	−25.5%	1,212	2,150	56%	62	2.3%
Mauritius	10,017	4.0%	–	81.6%	32.6%	5,332	14,736	36%	8	0.7%
Mexico	9,023	1.4%	53.1	60.8%	223.4%	4,978	13,152	38%	503	0.5%
Moldova	2,109	−9.5%	40.6	96.8%	–	1,680	2,577	65%	474	11.0%
Mongolia	1,783	−0.3%	33.2	93.4%	–	1,430	2,135	67%	8	0.3%
Morocco	3,546	0.6%	39.5	56.7%	30.4%	2,019	5,068	40%	24	0.1%
Mozambique	854	3.9%	39.6	35.6%	–	705	1,007	70%	366	2.0%
Namibia	6,431	1.8%	–	85.2%	–	4,413	8,498	52%	115	6.6%
Nepal	1,327	2.4%	36.7	43.2%	127.1%	880	1,752	50%	489	2.1%
Netherlands	25,657	2.2%	32.6	112.5%	44.4%	17,635	33,822	52%	1,430	9.0%
New Zealand	20,070	1.8%	–	54.5%	67.5%	16,203	24,052	67%	845	22.4%
Nicaragua	2,366	0.6%	60.3	100.9%	65.2%	1,431	3,310	43%	27	0.5%
Niger	746	−1.0%	50.5	0.3%	−46.9%	542	947	57%	119	1.1%
Nigeria	896	−0.4%	50.6	80.3%	−39.9%	532	1,254	42%	744	0.7%
Norway	29,918	3.1%	25.8	58.4%	14.8%	23,454	36,510	64%	251	5.6%
Oman	–	0.3%	–	74.8%	–	3,806	21,804	17%	682	26.9%
Pakistan	1,928	1.2%	31.2	32.8%	−13.3%	916	2,884	32%	2,242	1.6%
Panama	6,000	2.3%	48.5	42.9%	–	3,960	8,004	49%	81	2.8%
Papua New Guinea	2,280	1.4%	50.9	81.2%	−7.5%	1,670	2,840	59%	17	0.4%
Paraguay	4,426	−0.4%	57.7	40.5%	142.3%	2,155	6,658	32%	203	3.7%
Peru	4,799	2.9%	46.2	29.5%	45.9%	1,950	7,695	25%	45	0.2%
Philippines	3,971	1.1%	46.2	98.5%	142.3%	2,933	4,994	59%	160	0.2%
Poland	9,051	4.5%	31.6	51.1%	–	6,936	11,288	61%	2,087	5.4%
Portugal	17,290	2.5%	35.6	58.6%	118.5%	12,134	22,850	53%	232	2.3%
Qatar	–	–	–	–	–	6,864	25,277	27%	409	72.5%
Romania	6,423	−0.4%	31.1	63.8%	–	4,751	8,169	58%	92	0.4%

Sources: **Col 1** UNDP, *Human Development Report 2002* Indicator 12; **Col 2** World Bank, *World Development Indicators 2002* 2.8 ; **Col 3** World Bank, *World Development Indicators 2002* 6.1; **Col 4** UNDP, *Human Development Report 2002* Indicator 22; **Col 5** <www.un.org/esa/population>

Economics and the Environment

6 Military spending		7 Armed forces	8 Refugees and asylum seekers	9 Energy			10 Motor vehicles	11 Water use	Countries
per person 2001 US$	as % of GDP 2001	excluding opposition forces 2001	Number in host country 2002	Amount used per person 2000 equivalent of tonne of oil	CO_2 released 2000 million tonnes	CO_2 released per person 2000 tonnes	Number per 1,000 people 2000 or latest available data	Liters per person per day 2002	
2,514	12.1%	15,500	50,000	10.5	63	32	–	1,387	Kuwait
51	2.0%	9,000	9,700	0.5	4.6	0.9	39	770	Kyrgyzstan
4	0.9%	29,100	–	–	–	–	9	5,615	Laos
35	1.2%	6,500	–	1.5	6.5	2.8	260	514	Latvia
160	3.5%	71,830	389,500	1.2	14	3.3	336	323	Lebanon
11	3.1%	2,000	–	–	–	–	11	1,013	Lesotho
8	5.6%	13,000	60,000	–	–	–	15	67	Liberia
101	4.1%	76,000	33,000	3.1	39	7.3	–	122	Libya
57	1.8%	12,190	–	1.9	11	3	322	2,382	Lithuania
332	0.8%	900	–	8.4	8	18	–	188	Luxembourg
36	2.2%	16,000	–	1.4	8.4	4.1	132	–	Macedonia
3	1.0%	13,500	–	2.1	106	4.6	6	–	Madagascar
0	0.3%	5,300	6,000	–	–	–	4	2,796	Malawi
144	3.8%	100,500	57,500	–	–	–	200	227	Malaysia
5	2.5%	7,350	9,000	–	–	–	4	1,570	Mali
60	0.7%	2,140	–	2.1	2.3	5.8	–	328	Malta
9	2.9%	15,650	25,000	–	–	–	9	391	Mauritania
7	0.2%	–	–	–	–	–	98	1,676	Mauritius
57	0.9%	192,770	6,200	1.6	360	3.7	151	849	Mexico
34	1.7%	8,228	–	0.7	6.4	1.5	70	2,156	Moldova
9	2.4%	9,100	–	–	–	–	30	1,890	Mongolia
1,089	4.2%	198,500	–	0.4	29	1	52	463	Morocco
4	1.9%	11,000	5,000	0.4	1.2	0.1	–	1,013	Mozambique
51	3.1%	9,000	31,000	0.6	1.9	1.1	0	91	Namibia
6	2.7%	46,000	131,000	0.3	3	0.1	–	388	Nepal
394	1.7%	50,430	31,000	4.8	177	11	427	3,442	Netherlands
175	1.4%	9,230	–	4.9	32	8.3	540	1,349	New Zealand
5	1.1%	16,000	–	0.5	3.5	0.7	10	1,450	Nicaragua
3	1.8%	5,300	–	–	–	–	6	694	Niger
4	1.3%	78,500	7,000	0.7	43	0.3	33	126	Nigeria
659	1.8%	26,700	13,200	5.7	34	7.5	505	87	Norway
1,089	14.4%	43,400	–	4.1	24	9.8	130	1,244	Oman
17	4.4%	620,000	2,018,000	0.5	98	0.7	8	1,320	Pakistan
46	1.3%	–	–	0.9	4.9	1.7	113	3,018	Panama
5	0.9%	4,400	5,400	–	–	–	–	1,576	Papua New Guinea
14	1.1%	18,600	–	0.7	3.3	0.6	–	57	Paraguay
34	1.7%	100,000	–	0.5	26	1	43	214	Peru
14	1.5%	107,000	–	0.6	69	0.9	31	2,026	Philippines
88	2.0%	206,045	–	2.3	293	7.6	286	2,007	Poland
223	2.0%	43,600	–	2.5	60	6	348	871	Portugal
2,072	7.1%	12,330	–	26.8	35	60	–	1,994	Qatar
43	2.5%	103,000	–	1.6	86	3.9	154	1,380	Romania

Col 6 *The Military Balance 2002*; **Col 7** *The Military Balance 2002*; **Col 8** US Committee for Refugees, *World Refugee Survey 2002*; **Col 9** International Energy Agency: *Key World Statistics 2002* <www.iea.org/statist/keyworld2002>; **Col 10** World Bank, *World Development Indicators 2002*; **Col 11** FAO Aquastats <www.fao.org>

Countries	1 Gross Domestic Product		2 Wealth distribution	3 Trade		4 Earnings			5 Migrants excluding refugees	
	per person 2000 Purchasing Power Parity US$	annual % change 1999–2000	measured by Gini index (0 = equality) 1990s	as % of GDP 2000	% change as share of GDP 1980–99	Women's average annual earnings 2000 US$	Men's average annual earnings 2000 US$	Women's earnings as % of men's earnings 2000	Number 2000	% of population 2000
Russia	8,377	−4.6%	48.7	60.0%	–	6,611	10,383	64%	13,233	9.1%
Rwanda	943	−2.1%	28.9	14.8%	97.7%	760	1,130	67%	61	0.8%
Samoa	5,041	1.9%	–	–	–	–	–	–	8	5.0%
Saudi Arabia	11,367	−1.2%	–	66.0%	–	3,466	18,252	19%	5,250	25.8%
Senegal	1,510	0.9%	41.3	56.8%	−21.0%	1,074	1,949	55%	263	2.8%
Seychelles	–	1.1%	–	0.0%	0.0%	–	–	–	5	5.7%
Sierra Leone	490	−6.5%	62.9	32.0%	−62.6%	–	–	–	40	0.9%
Singapore	23,356	4.7%	–	295.3%	–	15,433	31,167	50%	1,352	33.6%
Slovakia	11,243	1.9%	19.5	128.5%	–	8,903	13,715	65%	32	0.6%
Slovenia	17,367	2.8%	28.4	103.9%	–	13,327	21,642	62%	48	2.4%
Solomon Islands	1,648	−1.0%	–	–	–	–	–	–	4	0.8%
Somalia	–	–	–	–	–	–	–	–	21	0.2%
South Africa	9,401	–	59.3	–	23.2%	5,888	13,024	45%	1,287	3.0%
Spain	19,472	2.3%	32.5	47.8%	154.6%	11,791	27,503	43%	1,252	3.1%
Sri Lanka	3,530	3.9%	34.4	73.3%	40.1%	2,270	4,724	48%	397	2.1%
Sudan	1,797	5.6%	–	28.7%	−32.2%	847	2,736	31%	365	1.2%
Suriname	3,799	3.0%	–	–	–	2,557	6,479	39%	6	1.5%
Swaziland	4,492	0.2%	60.9	131.2%	38.1%	–	–	–	41	4.4%
Sweden	24,277	1.6%	25.0	70.3%	67.1%	19,690	28,961	68%	835	9.4%
Switzerland	28,769	0.2%	33.1	68.9%	50.6%	19,197	38,550	50%	1,743	24.3%
Syria	3,556	2.8%	–	47.8%	−31.7%	1,537	5,522	28%	512	3.2%
Tajikistan	1,152	−11.8%	34.7	146.8%	–	872	1,434	61%	315	5.2%
Tanzania	523	0.1%	38.2	24.2%	–	436	611	71%	212	0.6%
Thailand	6,402	3.3%	41.4	107.2%	99.5%	4,907	7,928	62%	248	0.4%
Togo	1,442	−0.4%	–	73.0%	−22.3%	927	1,964	47%	167	3.7%
Trinidad & Tobago	8,964	2.3%	40.3	107.4%	43.7%	5,532	12,432	44%	41	3.2%
Tunisia	6,363	3.0%	41.7	74.0%	9.3%	3,347	9,320	36%	37	0.4%
Turkey	6,974	2.1%	41.5	40.0%	–	4,379	9,516	46%	1,500	2.2%
Turkmenistan	3,956	−8.0%	40.8	93.1%	–	–	–	–	208	4.4%
Uganda	1,208	3.8%	37.4	32.9%	–	966	1,451	67%	292	1.3%
Ukraine	3,816	−8.8%	29.0	89.7%	–	2,716	5,085	53%	6,944	14.0%
United Arab Emirates	17,935	−1.6%	–	119.9%	–	5,320	24,412	22%	1,921	73.7%
United Kingdom	23,509	2.2%	36.8	43.9%	55.6%	17,931	29,264	61%	3,908	6.6%
United States of America	34,142	2.2%	40.8	20.7%	99.1%	26,259	42,246	62%	34,480	12.2%
Uruguay	9,035	2.6%	42.3	29.2%	90.9%	6,178	12,068	51%	88	2.7%
Uzbekistan	2,441	−2.4%	44.7	75.9%	–	1,931	2,958	65%	1,329	5.3%
Venezuela	5,794	−0.6%	49.5	39.7%	12.1%	3,334	8,223	41%	1,006	4.2%
Vietnam	1,996	6.0%	36.1	96.0%	–	1,635	2,360	69%	6	0.0%
Yemen	893	2.3%	33.4	83.1%	–	405	1,384	29%	188	1.0%
Yugoslavia	–	–	–	64.2%	–	–	–	–	142	1.3%
Zambia	780	−2.1%	52.6	54.3%	−45.1%	562	995	56%	127	1.2%
Zimbabwe	2,635	0.4%	50.1	44.9%	139.6%	1,946	3,324	59%	652	5.2%

 Sources: Col 1 UNDP, *Human Development Report 2002* Indicator 12; **Col 2** World Bank, *World Development Indicators 2002* 2.8 ; **Col 3** World Bank, *World Development Indicators 2002* 6.1; **Col 4** UNDP, *Human Development Report 2002* Indicator 22; **Col 5** <www.un.org/esa/population>

Economics and the Environment

6 Military spending		7 Armed forces	8 Refugees and asylum seekers	9 Energy			10 Motor vehicles	11 Water use	Countries
per person 2001 US$	as % of GDP 2001	excluding opposition forces 2001	Number in host country 2002	Amount used per person 2000 equivalent of tonne of oil	CO_2 released 2000 million tonnes	CO_2 released per person 2000 tonnes	Number per 1,000 people 2000 or latest available data	Liters per person per day 2002	
440	4.3%	977,100	–	4.2	1506	10	153	3,175	Russia
12	5.8%	65,000	35,000	–	–	–	2	1,452	Rwanda
–	–	–	–	–	–	–		277	Samoa
1,156	14.1%	126,500	128,500	5.1	261	13	165	–	Saudi Arabia
6	1.4%	9,700	43,000	0.3	3.6	0.4	11	2,292	Senegal
142	1.8%	450	–	–	–	–	–	396	Seychelles
3	1.7%	6,000	15,000	–	–	–	3	–	Sierra Leone
1,044	5.1%	60,500	–	6.1	42	10	132	230	Singapore
71	2.0%	33,000	–	3.2	38	7	260	–	Slovakia
139	1.5%	7,600	–	3.3	14	7.3	455	903	Slovenia
–	–	–	–	–	–	–	–	682	Solomon Islands
4	4.4%	–	–	–	–	–	2	–	Somalia
41	1.7%	61,500	22,000	2.5	296	6.9	143	253	South Africa
174	1.2%	143,450	–	3.1	285	7.1	472	842	Spain
41	5.1%	121,000	–	0.4	11	0.6	34	2,111	Sri Lanka
18	4.3%	117,000	307,000	0.5	5.7	0.2	9	1,414	Sudan
58	5.3%	2,040	18,500	–	–	–	–	1,568	Suriname
–	–	33,900	57,900	–	–	–	70	3,021	Swaziland
443	1.9%	3,600	397,600	5.4	52	5.9	478	1,943	Sweden
394	1.2%	321,000	–	3.7	42	5.8	526	908	Switzerland
114	10.9%	370,000	–	1.1	52	3.2	30	455	Syria
21	1.7%	6,000	–	0.5	4.4	0.7	3	2,439	Tajikistan
4	1.6%	27,000	498,000	0.5	1.6	0.1	5	5,344	Tanzania
29	1.7%	306,000	277,000	1.2	147	2.4	46	91	Thailand
7	2.5%	9,450	11,000	0.3	1.3	0.3	24	1,445	Togo
52	0.8%	2,700	–	6.7	15	12	–	55	Trinidad & Tobago
39	1.9%	35,000	–	0.8	18	1.9	48	629	Tunisia
107	5.0%	515,100	12,600	1.2	204	3.1	85	891	Turkey
46	2.6%	17,500	14,000	2.7	34	6.6	–	1,299	Turkmenistan
5	2.2%	55,000	174,000	–	–	–	5	13,752	Uganda
100	2.2%	303,800	6,000	2.8	301	6.1	65	24	Ukraine
1,137	4.6%	65,000	–	10.2	69	24	121	1,437	United Arab Emirates
583	2.5%	211,430	69,800	3.9	531	8.9	418	2,216	United Kingdom
1,128	3.2%	1,367,700	492,500	8.4	5665	21	760	544	United States of America
103	2.0%	23,900	–	0.9	5.3	1.6	174	4,521	Uruguay
70	2.6%	53,000	38,000	2.0	115	4.6	–	534	Uzbekistan
77	1.5%	82,300	–	2.5	129	5.3	–	6,392	Venezuela
30	7.2%	484,000	16,000	0.5	41	0.5	–	465	Vietnam
28	8.1%	54,000	69,500	0.2	9.2	0.5	34	1,905	Yemen
58	6.3%	105,500	400,000	1.3	43	4.1	190	438	Yugoslavia
3	0.8%	21,600	270,000	0.6	1.7	0.2	15	–	Zambia
23	2.9%	39,000	9,000	0.8	13	1.1	–	449	Zimbabwe

Col 6 *The Military Balance 2002*; **Col 7** *The Military Balance 2002*; **Col 8** US Committee for Refugees, *World Refugee Survey 2002*; **Col 9** International Energy Agency: *Key World Statistics 2002* <www.iea.org/statist/keyworld2002>; **Col 10** World Bank, *World Development Indicators 2002*; **Col 11** FAO Aquastats <www.fao.org>

Sources

Part 1 Power
World Fact
UNDP, *Human Development Report 2002*, (Oxford and New York: OUP) p1

12–13 POLITICAL SYSTEMS
The author

14–15 CONTROL OF THE SEAS
The Law of the Sea
United Nations: *Oceans: The Source of Life*, 2002
<www.un.org/Depts/los/convention_agreements/
convention_20years/oceanssourceoflife.pdf>

Ownership of warships worldwide
Dan Smith, *The Atlas of War and Peace* (New York: Penguin and London: Earthscan, 2003)

Offshore oil production
United Nations: *Oceans: The Source of Life*, 2002
<www.un.org/Depts/los/convention_agreements/
convention_20years/oceanssourceoflife.pdf>

Piracy on the high seas
<home.wanadoo.nl/m.bruyneel/archive/modern/figures.htm>
International Marine Organization MSC.4/Circular 30 (7 February 2003) <www.imo.org/Circulars/>
United Nations: *Oceans: The Source of Life*, 2002
<www.un.org/Depts/los/convention_agreements/
convention_20years/oceanssourceoflife.pdf>

16–17 CONTROL OF SPACE
Jonathan McDowell: Jonathan's Space Home Page
<hea-www.harvard.edu/QEDT/jcm/space/jsr/jsr.html>

18–19 INTERNATIONAL ORGANIZATIONS
Websites of the organizations covered

GDP of G8 countries
World Development Indicators 2002, Table 1.1 (Washington DC: The World Bank, 2002)

20–21 TRANSNATIONALS
Transnationalization
UNCTAD, *The World Investment Report 2002*, Annex tables A.1.6 Transnationality, Index of host economies, 1999
The index combines data on the importance of foreign direct investment in a country's economy, and the significance of foreign companies in terms of Gross Domestic Product and employment. For the purposes of the map the following classification has been devised:
very important: 40.0 – 100
important: 20.0 – 39.9
moderately important 10.0 – 19.9
not very important 5.0 – 9.9
unimportant 0 – 4.9

Home base of top 100 TNCs
op cit, Table IV.I, pp85-87

Foreign direct investment
op cit, Annex table A.I.1, p265
World fact
op cit, p.90

22–23 SUPERPOWER
International Institute for Strategic Studies, *The Military Balance 2002–2003* (New York and Oxford: Oxford University Press)
<http://www3.oup.co.uk/milbal/contents/>

Part 2 The Cost of Living
UN, *World Urbanization Prospects, The 1999 Revision* (New York, 2000)

26–27 POPULATION
Population size
UNStats Social Indicators
<unstats.un.org/unsd/demographic/social/population.htm>

Future populations
<www.census.gov/ipc/<www/idbpyr.html>

28–29 URBANIZATION
People living in cities
UN Stats Database: Social Indicators:
<unstats.un.org/unsd/demographic/social/hum-set.htm>

Megacities
Urban populations
Urban populations in 2015
United Nations Population Division: *World Urbanization Prospects: The 2001 Revision*
<www.un.org/esa/population/>

30–31 TRAFFIC
Motor vehicles
World Development Indicators 2002, Table 3.12 (Washington DC: The World Bank, 2002)

Relative safety
The World Bank
<www.worldbank.org/transport/roads/safety/htm>

The growing number of cars
WorldWatch: *Vital Signs 1999–2000*, and *Vital Signs 2002* (London: Earthscan)

World facts
Cited by *Guardian Society* 26 March 2002, page 8, in article by Jonathan Whitelegg, co-editor of *Earthscan Reader in World Transport Policy and Practice* (London: Earthscan)

32–33 ENERGY
Energy consumption
World energy production
World energy consumption
International Energy Agency: *Key World Energy Statistics 2002*
<www.iea.org/statist/keyworld2002/keyworld2002.pdf>

34–35 CLIMATE CHANGE
Greenhouse gases
International Energy Agency: *Key World Statistics 2002*
<www.iea.org/statist/keyworld2002>

Temperature change graphic
Climatic Research Unit, Univ of East Anglia, UK
<www.cru.uea.ac.uk/cru/data/temperature/>

Antarctic
Websites of:
British Antarctic Survey
NASA
National Science Foundation

36–37 BIODIVERSITY
Forests
FAO data via UNEP GeoData Portal

Threatened Species
IUCN – World Conservation Union Red List
<www.redlist.org/info/tables/table1.html>

38–39 WATER
FAO Aquastat database:

Wages for water
The cost of hygiene
Guardian Special Issue, August 2002

Part 3 Differences
The Linguasphere Register of the World's Languages and Speech
Communities <www.linguasphere.org/register.html>

42–43 QUALITY OF LIFE
Relative human development
UNDP, *Human Development Report 2002*, Table 1 (Oxford and
New York: OUP)
Classification used:
very high: 900 points and above
high: 800–899 points
medium: 500–799 points
low: 400–499 points
very low: under 400 points

Up and downs
<www.undp.org/hdr2002/presskit/>

44–44 ETHNICITY
Dan Smith, *The Atlas of War and Peace* (New York: Penguin and
London: Earthscan, 2003)
Dan Smith, The State of the World Atlas (New York and London:
Penguin, 1999)

46–47 BELIEFS
based on: Joanne O'Brien and Martin Palmer *The State of
Religion Atlas* (New York: Simon & Schuster, 1993). Checked and
updated by the authors 2002

48–49 RICH AND POOR
Disparities
World Development Indicators 2002, Table 2.8 (Washington DC:
The World Bank, 2002)

How the cookie crumbles
UNDP, *Human Development Report 2002*, Table 4 (Oxford and
New York: OUP)

50–51 LITERACY
Illiteracy
Illiteracy rates converted from literacy rates presented in UNDP,
Human Development Report, 2002 Table 10 (Oxford and New
York: OUP)

Symbol – computed from UNESCO illiteracy stats on UNESCO
Institute for Statistics website

World fact
UNESCO statistic

Functional illiteracy
UNDP, *Human Development Report 2002* Table 4 (Oxford and
New York: OUP)

Primary school enrolment
UNESCO Institute for Statistics website

52–53 WORKPLACES
Dominant employment sector
International Labour Organization, Key Indicators of the Labour
Market: 4. Employment by Sector
<www.ilo.org/public/english/employment/strat/kilm/kilm04.htm>

Wealth and employment
UNDP, *Human Development Report 2002*, Table 1 (Oxford and
New York: OUP)

Hours of work graphic
<www.ilo.org/public/english/employment/strat/kilm/table.htm>
Comparison of working hours US and UK cited by Charlotte
Denny, March 17, 2003 *The Guardian*

Part 4 Rights
Human Rights Watch <www.hrw.org/un/chr59/omnibus.htm>

56–57 HUMAN RIGHTS
Extreme abuse of human rights
Judicial killings
Executions in 2001
Amnesty International Reports 1998–2002 inclusive

58–59 FREE SPEECH
Freedom of the press
A dangerous profession
Press freedom
Leonard R Sussman & Karin Deutsch Karlekar, *The Annual
Survey of Press Freedom 2002*, New York, Freedom House, 2001
<www.freedomhouse.org>

60–61 CHILDREN'S RIGHTS
Infantry
Dan Smith, *The Atlas of War and Peace* (New York: Penguin
and London: Earthscan, 2003)

Child labor
<www.ilo.org/ilolex/english/docs/declworld.htm>

Birth registration
UNICEF: *State of the World's Children, 2001* (New York: UNICEF, 2001)

62–63 SEXUAL FREEDOM
Homosexuality and the law
International Lesbian and Gay Rights Association legal survey <www.ilga.org/Information/Legal_survey/>

Homosexual rights around the world
<http://www.actwin.com/eatonohio/gay/world.htm>

Cost of condoms
Restrictions on women's sexuality
Joni Seager: *The Penguin Atlas of Women in the World* (New York: Penguin, 2003)
published in the UK as *The Atlas of Women* (London: The Women's Press, 2003)

64–65 RELIGIOUS FREEDOM
based on: Joanne O'Brien and Martin Palmer *The State of Religion Atlas* (New York: Simon & Schuster, 1993). Checked and updated by the authors 2002

66–67 WOMEN'S RIGHTS
Employment
Calculated from UNDP, *Human Development Report 2002*, Table 22 (Oxford and New York: OUP)
Maternity pay from:
Joni Seager: *The Penguin Atlas of Women in the World* (New York: Penguin, 2003), published in the UK as *The Atlas of Women*, (London: The Women's Press, 2003)

Abortion and the law
Center for Reproductive Law and Policy (NY), *The World's Abortion Laws 2000*

Part 5: Control
Dan Smith, *The Atlas of War and Peace* (New York: Penguin and London: Earthscan, 2003)

70–71 WAR
Wars since the Cold War
World news media sources

Anti-personnel mines
Landmine monitor 2002 <www.icbl.org/lm/2002/findings/html>

72–73 TERRORISM
Rand-MIPT Terrorist Incident Database: (Rand Corporation, Santa Monica, Ca & Oklahoma City National Memorial Institute for the Prevention of Terrorism, 2003)
<db.mipt.org/mipt_rand.cfm>
Designated Foreign Terrorist Organizations (U.S. State Department
Office of Counterterrorism, 9 August 2002: US Department of State International Information Programs)
<usinfo.state.gov/topical/pol/terror/>
Center for Defense Information Terrorism Project: (CDI, Washington, DC) <www.cdi.org/terrorism/>
News media reports

74–75 MILITARY SPENDING
Spending priorities
Budgeting for war
International Institute for Strategic Studies, *The Military Balance 2002–2003*, Table 26 (New York and Oxford: OUP)

Health expenditure
World Development Indicators 2002, Table 2.15 (Washington DC: The World Bank, 2002)

76–77 ARMED FORCES
Under arms

Armed opposition groups
International Institute for Strategic Studies, *The Military Balance 2002–2003*, Table 26 (New York and Oxford: OUP)

Women in regular armed forces
individual country sources

78–79 PEACEKEEPING
Forces for peace
UN Peacekeeping Operations
<www.un.org/Depts/dpko/dpko/ops.htm>

80–82 REFUGEES
US Committee for Refugees, *World Refugee Survey 2002* <www.refugees.org/world/worldmain.htm>

Part 6: Money
Suzanne Elston, ENN, January 31, 2001, quoting Institute for Policy Studies
<www.enn.com/news>

32 NATIONAL ECONOMY
Purchasing Power
UNDP, Human Development Report 2002 Table 1 (Oxford and New York: OUP, 2002)

Inflation
op cit Table 12

33 TRADE AND INDUSTRY
The importance of trade
Change in trade
World Development Indicators 2002, Table 6.1 (Washington DC: The World Bank, 2002)

Bloc trade
UNCTAD Statistics in brief <www.unctad.org>

Unfair trade
World Development Indicators 2002, Table 6.4 (Washington DC: The World Bank, 2002)

88–89 DEBT AND AID
Debt servicing
Overseas development aid received
UNDP, *Human Development Report 2002* Table 16 (Oxford and New York: OUP)

Overseas development assistance
UNDP, *Human Development Report 2002* Table 15 (Oxford and New York: OUP)

35 DRUGS TRADE
Trading in narcotics
Global Illicit Drug Trends 2002 (Research Section of the United Nations International Drug Control Programme (UNDCP), United Nations Office on Drugs and Crime (UNODC))
<www.odccp.org/odccp/global_illicit_drug_trends.html>
International Narcotics Control Strategy Report 2002 (US State Department, Bureau for International Narcotics and Law Enforcement Affairs) <www.state.gov/g/inl/>
<www.theantidrug.com/drugs_terror/drug_sources.html>
<www.pbs.org/wgbh/pages/frontline/shows/drugs/business/map.html>

Illicit growth
Drugs of choice
Drugs trade profit margins
World fact
Global Illicit Drug Trends 2002, Research Section of the United Nations International Drug Control Programme (UNDCP), United Nations Office on Drugs and Crime (UNODC)
<www.odccp.org/odccp/global_illicit_drug_trends.html>

36 MIGRANT WORKERS
Cross-border migration
Sending money home
Number of migrants
Data table and Press Release on migrants from UN Population Division Department of Economic and Social Affairs
<www.un.org/esa/population>

Part 7: The Business of Pleasure
World fact
World Resources Institute

96–97 COMMUNICATIONS
Phones
<www.itu.int/ITU-D/ict/statistics/at_glance/main01.pdf>
<www.itu.int/ITU-D/ict/statistics/at_glance/cellular01.pdf>

Internet users worldwide
<www.itu.int/ITU-D/ict/statistics/at_glance/KeyTelecom99.html>
The Observer, 30 March 2003

Personal computers
<www.itu.int/ITU-D/ict/statistics/at_glance/Internet01.pdf>

World fact
Text messages, *Daily Mirror*, 6 February 2002

98–99 MEDIA
Watching television
World Development Indicators 2002 Table 5.10 (Washington DC: The World Bank, 2002)

Media moguls
<www.pbs.org/wgbh/pages/frontline/shows/hollywood/business/rev.html>

Hollywood and Bollywood
<www.rediff.com/movies/2003/jan/30bolly.htm>

100–101 SPORT
Football World Cup 2002
<www.kirchsport.com/inhalt/news/news_details.asp?id=92>
<fifaworldcup.yahoo.com/en020624/2/17xw.html>

Nike's increasing sales
Nike's factories
Richard M Locke, Alvin J Siteman, The Promise and Perils of Globalization: The Case of Nike (MIT)
<mitsloan.mit.edu/50th/nikepaper.pdf>

Value of Sydney Olympics
<www.business.nsw.gov.au/facts>

Ball games
<www.manutdzone.com/atoz/w.html>

102–103 TRAVEL AND TOURISM
Tourism dependency
Tourists
Destinations
World Development Indicators 2002 Table 6.14 (Washington DC: The World Bank, 2002)

104–105 SEX TRADE
Joni Seager: *The Penguin Atlas of Women in the World*, Penguin, New York, 2003
published in the UK as *The Atlas of Women*, Earthscan, London 2003

World Fact
UN quoted by *Observer* 23 June 2002

UK fact
European Parliament, 2002

Viagra
Pfizer website

Online pornography
in USA
eMarketer report quoted by nua
<www.nua.ie/surveys/index>

Hardcore video titles
Adult Video News, December 2001; Jupiter Media Metrix; Nielsen/Net Ratings

Part 8 Life and Death
World Bank, *World Development Report 2000/2001* (New York: Oxford University Press, 2000), p23

108–109 LIFE EXPECTANCY
Life expectancy at birth
Changing life expectancy
UNDP, *Human Development Report 2002* Table 8 (Oxford and New York: OUP)

Water supplies
UNDP, *Human Development Report 2002* Table 3 (Oxford and New York: OUP)

Causes of death
WHO Report 2002 Annex Table 2 (Geneva: World Health Organization) <who.org/int/en>

110–111 MALNUTRITION
<www.fao.org/english/newsroom/news/2002/9703-en.html>
<www.who.int/vaccines-diseases/en/viatmina/advocacy/adv05.shtml>

Hungry children
UNICEF/WHO data on UNStats Millennium Indicators website
Undernourished adults
FAO data on UNStats Millennium Indicators website

Malnourished and vulnerable
WHO Report 2002 Annex Table 2 (Geneva: World Health
Organization) <who.org/int/en>

112–113 HIV/AIDS
People infected with HIV/AIDS
UNAIDS: Table of country-specific HIV/AIDS estimates and data,
end 2001 (published August 2002)
<www.unaids.org/barcelona/>

Death rate
Living with HIV/AIDS
Text boxes
UNAIDS: AIDS epidemic update (published December 2002)
<www.unaids.org/worldaidsday/2002/press/Epiupdate.html>

114–115 MENTAL HEALTH
<www.befrienders.org/suicide/statistics.htm>
World Health Organization, *Facts and Figures about Suicide*
(Geneva: WHO, 1999)

Who commits suicide
Suicide rates among men
Suicide rates among women
<www5.who.int/mental_health/main.cfm?p=0000000149>

Mental health resources
Department of Mental Health and Substance Dependence, WHO,
Geneva

Antidepressant sales
<www.ims-global.com>

116–117 SMOKING
Judith Mackay & Michael Eriksen, *The Tobacco Atlas* (Geneva:
World Health Organization, 2002)
<www.tfn.net/HealthGazette/smoke.html>

Past and future
Tobacco deaths among men
Tobacco deaths among women
M Ezzati & A Lopez 'Mortality and burden of disease
attributable to smoking and oral tobacco use, Global and
Regional estimates for 2000', *Comparative Risk Assessment*,
(Geneva: World Health Organization, 2002)

Global cigarette consumption
A P McGinn, 'The Nicotine Cartel', *World Watch*, Vol 10, no4;
Worldwatch Institute, 1997: 18–27

Commercial interest
Tobacco industry estimates obtained by Mackay and Eriksen

118–119 RICH LIVING
WHO Report 2002, Annex Table 6 (Geneva: World Health
Organization, 2002)

PHOTO CREDITS

Index